£2

THE RISE AN
THE NINE O'CL

A Cult Within the Church?

ROLAND HOWARD

MOWBRAY

Mowbray
A Cassell imprint
Wellington House, 125 Strand, London WC2R 0BB
127 West 24th Street, New York, NY 10011

First published 1996

British Library Cataloguing-in-Publication Data
A catalogue record for this book is available from the British Library.

ISBN 0 264 67419 7

Printed and bound in Great Britain
by Biddles Ltd, Guildford and King's Lynn.

Contents

Addendum

Page 129 line 24

"At that stage, the press were not involved, but the community were anxious about the possibility of the media descending on them and Lowe was still uncertain about the full extent of what had happened. However, Jennings advised that once proper pastoral care had been arranged for all concerned, the Diocese should issue a full statement on the following Monday, or earlier if the press asked about NOS. Following that, a policy of complete openness with the media would be essential."

Introduction

Before the Nine O'Clock Service (NOS) hit the headlines in August 1995, the story was a radical nightclub-style Church of England, raving in the aisles. Then in the media frenzy the story was a Randy Vicar story; a Randy Vicar story on an unprecedented level, involving a score of women and spiced up by bikini-clad dancers performing in services. The real story is more disturbing.

NOS was a Church of England flagship congregation not simply because of its experimental worship, which resembled a state-of-the-art nightclub with film loops, projections, multi-track mixing desks and 'attitude', but also because of its radical state-of-the-art 'post-modern' theology. Here was a church facing squarely the issues that other churches ignored: poverty; racism; sexuality; and the environmental crisis. Here was a church reaching out intelligently to a 'godless generation', bringing them Christianity with a passion for, and commitment to, their issues. NOS was refreshing the parts that other churches couldn't reach.

Yet two of NOS's rave service film loops inadvertently betrayed a deeper reality. One was of a fish washed up and floundering in the shallows of a polluted stream, struggling for survival. The other is a computer-generated image of going through a never-ending series of doors, going deeper and deeper inside, but getting nowhere. Both are resonant symbols of what life was like for members of the congregation. To exist in NOS involved being 'vortexed' through increasingly strange doors of perception, deeper into a controlling organisation. It was a struggle for survival and the stream was poisoned.

Underneath the carefully manicured exterior, the real story is of a man who seemed, according to many, to have a megalomaniac desire to control other people; of a complex, secretive organisation, where unknown to many, abuse existed; of a leadership convinced that their leader was God's mouthpiece who was going to save Western civilisation. Yet it is also clear that the Revd Chris Brain was no mere pantomime villain. The 'vision' that he held out to his congregation was intelligent and relevant, and although most members I interviewed believe that he behaved cynically and cruelly, others point to a struggle within him between his passion for justice and his desire for power. Some are convinced that his mission was genuine, while others suggest that he lost his way. Many are convinced that he was a skilful and ruthless power seeker.

The real story is of a congregation's sacrifice. The sacrifice of hundreds of thousands of pounds, of their careers, and of their minds, bodies, souls and dress sense to their enigmatic, charismatic and 'pure' leader. The real story is of lawyers, doctors, professors, psychiatrists, theologians, football fans and clubbers convinced that their leader was a prophet who could change the world.

The real story is of betrayal and abuse, of a leader living in luxury and travelling round the world in designer clothes whilst his congregation largely lived in the 'simple lifestyle'. It is of a minister, according to some, sexually involved with over 40 female members of his congregation. Moreover, it is of a priest manipulating, controlling and dominating the minds of several hundred members who thought he was ministering to them. The real story is about an insatiable desire for power, which was fulfilled by money and sexual involvement. This power was power to damn, power to humiliate, power to enter people's minds and power to control them. The real story is of a cult in the Church of England.

Central to every cult is a charismatic leader. Brain had the sort of charisma that could elicit massive financial gifts from followers to support his lifestyle; that could persuade young women to form a secretive team of handmaidens who started out by cleaning and shopping but ended up exploring sexual intimacy, convinced that he was ministering to them; that won plaudits from the Archbishop of Canterbury, and internationally known academics, and had senior Anglicans convinced that his radical approach and his church were the future for the Church of England. But, it was also the sort of charisma that made everyone freeze when he came in the room.

This is the story of Chris Brain and of his disciples, whose commitment and idealism were awesome and whose betrayal was devastating. This is a story of pioneering, visionary and relevant theology, corrupted into systematic abuse. But the Nine O'Clock Service is not only a story concerning abuse; it is also a story of integrity and idealism, of wrestling with the complexities and addictions of contemporary life as Christians. Many would say that it still has much to offer, now that their leader has been exposed. For most it was the importance and relevance of the church's vision that held their loyalty, and that made it harder to recognise the abuse. The corruption of the best, they say, is the worst.

Finally I would like to say that this book is not the whole story. Although it is intended to be the story of the NOS community, each individual has a different, frequently harrowing, tale to tell. Some stories have not been included in the interests of taste and sensitivity, others because of space. It has presented me with many difficult decisions as people try to put NOS behind them and start life anew. It has been a disturbing book to write.

It is with this in mind that the book is dedicated to the former members of the Nine O'Clock Service who have made themselves vulnerable at a time when they might have been tempted to silence. It is also dedicated to the integrity and idealism which fuelled their vision which, whatever its faults, will surely resonate with hope into the next millennium.

1

Origins of a Visionary

In many ways, as a young man Chris Brain was fairly unremarkable. Born in June 1957, he had a brother and sister and initially lived with both his parents. His father was a photographer and his mother worked in a shop in Harrogate. Brain told some who were close to him that he spent his childhood surrounded by beautiful women and, according to others, his father at some stage ran a modelling agency. He passed the eleven plus and attended the local school, Harrogate Granby High, where his behaviour has been variously described as quiet, confident, rebellious, deceptive and secretive.

Motorbikes were of greater interest than academic study, and he left school at the age of 17 with a 125cc motorbike and indifferent exam results. He was a 'member' of a motorbike gang and was known as quietly rebellious, a 'fly lad'. Another fairly typical teenage trait was getting into trouble. He told a friend that he had been sacked from working as a petrol pump attendant. Soon after leaving school, Brain became interested in Christianity through an old school friend, Roy Searle, who had been recently converted on a Christian retreat in Scotland.

According to Searle, Brain was a 'canny' character who was known as 'a good laugh' and who always had a questioning, radical streak. It was during his final year at school that Searle and Brain became friends, and Searle remembers him asking big questions about what direction his life was taking. Searle told him about his recent conversion and, over several months, Brain became interested in Christianity. It was on Bamburgh Beach, Northumberland, that he remembers Brain becoming a Christian. 'Chris experienced a quiet, but profound change', he says, 'he showed a genuine love for God.' Searle remembers a much gentler side to Brain's character emerging. They started attending a thriving youth group in Harrogate Baptist Church and Brain and Searle were soon involved in the leadership committee.

Brain's conversion was into the evangelical wing of the Christian Church, which is characterised by a belief that the bible is the inspired Word of God without error, and by an emphasis on an intense and personal relationship with Jesus. This personal relationship tends to focus on a conviction of personal sin, and receiving forgiveness for this sin, followed by a struggle to conquer it through prayer, bible study, good living and ongoing repentance, which should lead to holiness. Out of this intense and personal relationship comes the other characteristic of the movement, a desire to bring everyone to realise their need of the Saviour. The radical, life-changing conversion experience empowers this messianic vision to bring the world to repentance and life in relationship with Jesus, at which point the world's troubles will fall away.

Brain approached his faith with all the enthusiasm and seriousness of a young convert. He was baptised by full immersion (as a sign of becoming a new creation in Christ) in 1975 at the Baptist Church by the Revd Jack Pike. He took Christ's injunctions about helping the disadvantaged seriously and worked as a care assistant at a Red Cross home for the handicapped. Searle remembers the compassion and creativity with which he approached his work. Brain was liked by staff and patients. He also started telling friends and acquaintances about Christ. Clearly he had the charisma to bring others to faith.

One of the first people he made an impression on was Lynn Bulmer, a girl two years younger than him, from Harrogate Granby High School. Lynn was a quiet, studious girl and a talented musician. She played in the school orchestra and often played the piano in school assemblies and was a conventional, 'straight' and unassuming girl. It was a surprise to many of Lynn's friends when she became friendly with Brain, a long haired 'youth' with a motorbike. It was not long before Lynn was attending the Baptist Church with Brain and a number of his friends.

This friendship developed into romance and in August 1977 they were married at Harrogate Baptist Church. There were misgivings on the part of some relatives about the couple marrying so young, but it was seen by church members as a serious and positive step on their journey with God. The wedding was a tense occasion because the parents of both bride and groom had been divorced and remarried, but with his old school friend, Roy Searle, as best man and their evangelical friends to support them, Brain's marriage to Lynn (who later changed her name to Winnie) seemed a success and the couple moved into a flat in Harrogate.

During the following months, the Brains drifted away from the Baptist Church and started attending St Luke's, an Anglican church with livelier worship and charismatic leanings (the practice of spiritual gifts, whether prophecy, healing, or speaking in tongues). It was soon after the marriage that Brain believed that God had told him to start a rock band. The band was to be God's tool to bring young people to faith, to show young people that you didn't have to be 'square' to be a Christian. The band was called *Candescence* and made up of Brain and Winnie, and Pip Brain (Chris's brother) and had two roadies, Mark Estdale and Simon Towlson. When they needed a guitarist and backing singer, Jon Ingham, an eighteen-year-old enthusiast who had been deejaying and playing in punk rock bands for years, was asked to audition by Nina (not her real name), one of the band's growing entourage of helpers and supporters. He tells how he got half way through his audition and realised that punk rock wasn't what was needed, to play with *Candescence* he needed musical ability.

It was through talks with Nina that Ingham had become interested in Christianity. Initially Ingham had rejected Christianity, but Nina and Brain seemed to be reassuringly normal. After he spent some months toying with the idea, Brain brought him to the point of conversion. Ingham says: 'Chris brought me to faith, it was a major hold on me. He was my spiritual father, I understood the faith through him.' As the relationship deepened and grew, Ingham got Brain a job as a painter and decorator, and became *Candescence's* manager. Despite the fact that they were largely playing small youth clubs they took their work for *Candescence* seriously; it was, after all, 'God's work.' Ingham opened a bank account, they had minuted band meetings which always ended in prayer and they played wherever they were invited to.

Their commitment was such that they travelled widely for little or no money. On one occasion they travelled across the country to play at an outdoor evangelistic event at Great Salkeld, a tiny village in Cumbria. The outdoor event was rained off and they had to play in a small village hall to a dozen old ladies and just a handful of local youths. But their professionalism was such that they half filled the hall with meticulously set up equipment and played a full set. Although Winnie was the main musical force behind the group, Brain was the unstated leader and creative visionary. He took his work so seriously that he frequently asked Alastair Kendall, a slightly older member of St Luke's, if he would be willing to have 'spiritual oversight' of the band. Brain was a strong personality, and, perhaps realising this, he was asking for someone to be accountable to, Kendall declined.

The late David Watson, a respected Anglican charismatic, was a major influence on the band. His emphasis on a radical discipleship involving a simple lifestyle and a commitment to social justice was embraced by Brain and the band members. David Watson's church, St Michael-le-Belfrey, York, was experimenting in forms of income sharing to release members of the congregation for evangelistic work and this idea was later to take shape within the Nine O'Clock Service in Sheffield. They would sometimes visit St Michael-le-Belfrey, which was a thriving, radical and nationally known church. Watson's intellectual and articulate approach to Christianity presented them with their first vision of a radical, potentially world-changing picture of their faith, a faith which didn't hide from the complexity of contemporary culture. Watson was no pietistic fundamentalist; he was addressing the modern world with a thought out and apparently relevant charismatic approach.

Candescence were really non-conformist, radical Christians beginning to experiment with charismatic gifts (prophecy and speaking in tongues) who were seeking to promote this vision (which had changed their lives) to their generation which they saw as a lost culture. In 1978 Jon Ingham had a vision which he believed was prophetic. He saw a theatre full of people with a band playing ambient music in the darkness on the right and some performers centre stage, dressed as City gents walking inside a treadmill. The set was backed by a massive projection accompanied by a *sotto voce* narration. It was a picture of avant-garde performance art which was touring the country. Ingham's mother was in the audience and Jon was behind the audience organising the show. He told Brain about the vision and Brain left to talk to Winnie who had said that she'd had a strange dream. Brain returned saying that the vision and the dream were identical and that it must be a sign from God about their future. They were on a mission from God which demanded total commitment.

In 1978 Winnie Brain was accepted at Sheffield University on an honours degree course in music. The Brains settled in Crookes, a suburb to the west of the city and started attending St Thomas's, a thriving and strongly charismatic Anglican church led by the Revd Robert Warren. The band, and members of its entourage, settled in the same area and they renamed themselves *Present Tense*. Within a year Brain was a home group (a pastoral and bible study group) leader with Robert Warren in his group. Despite being members of St Thomas's, the band and its supporters were not uncritical of the church. They resented what they saw as the church's middle class values and attended Sunday services as a group sitting disgruntled at the back with their arms folded.

Yet the seriousness with which they approached their faith was demonstrated in more than just attitude. In 1978 Simon Towlson used a £20,000 inheritance to buy a house which he was to share with the Brains as the centre for the Christian community and the band. His commitment to a radical community lifestyle was such that he agreed to include the Brains on the title deeds of the house in Parkers Road. It was a demonstration of trust based on his understanding of early Christian values found in the New Testament. He bought the house, assuming that once it was sold the proceeds would be returned to him. At this time Ingham inherited about £50,000. His belief in the vision was such that he decided to donate it to *Candescence* (with some persuasion from Brain) despite objections from his family. The inheritance was taken as confirmation of Ingham's vision and the minutes of a band meeting in October 1978 note a request for prayer concerning the availability of the money and how it should be used. When the money finally arrived it was invested in state-of-the-art equipment to prepare them to fulfil the vision.

Despite these idealistic, if naive, beginnings, all was not as it seemed with *Candescence*. Estdale and Ingham have since discovered that before, and during, his marriage Brain had secret sexual encounters with members of the group. Mark Estdale's girlfriend had been involved with Brain, as had a singer who subsequently left. Brain had managed secretly to push a wedge between Estdale and his girlfriend, Nina, and to create mutual suspicion between her and Ingham, one of her oldest friends. Ingham was told that Nina was part of his 'old life' and was told to stop seeing her alone and to be suspicious of the motives behind her friendship with him. Brain's influence was such that Ingham was also instructed to give up his deejaying business as part of his discipleship. It was seen as part of his old life which he needed to give up. His equipment was donated to *Candescence*.

Mark Estdale also noted Brain's uncanny ability to 'read people' which he was later to use to devastating effect in the Nine O'Clock Service. He remembers Brain's outspoken criticism of a St Luke's youth leader and a prediction that he was being unfaithful to his wife and would leave her. 'He had only met the guy once', Estdale says, 'and he slated him severely.' Sometime later the youth leader left his wife for another woman. However, Estdale also remembers Brain more positively in the early years as 'a bit nutty'; he was exciting, passionate and energetic. He was an articulate dedicated catalyst but he was not without compassion. The likeable aspects of Brain's personality were also apparent to Ingham: 'Chris was a vibrant, active person, you never knew what he was going to do next. He also had a sharp sense of humour and a likeable charm. We took the good with the bad and accepted it.'

At this stage Brain and the band were exposed to dance music and fairly quickly adapted to the Sheffield dance and 'industrial' music scene. *Present Tense* (later named *Tense*) soon had a following of hundreds, mainly Christians, but they were fast developing credibility on the secular circuit. The vision at this stage was far more sophisticated. They eschewed the idea of overt evangelism as far too obvious and embarked on an avant-garde mission to infiltrate and subvert Western culture and thus to bring about more significant change by presenting radical Christian values which could make a long term, more substantial, difference. To get famous was to get themselves a 'prophetic platform' with which they could impact on contemporary culture.

They saw artists as the modern equivalent of biblical prophets because they were often at the formative edge of cultural development. Brain referred to the band as Urban Art Terrorists because their art was meant to seriously challenge Western culture with an enticing and radical alternative. 'Bomb in the back pocket' was the phrase Brain used of their relationship to the church because they were to get deeply involved with the church and then, at a later stage, reveal their true agenda and destroy the false middle class edifice which they saw as merely a spiritual reflection of worldly consumerism. Although in another sense the Nine O'Clock Service was to become a bomb in the Church of England's back pocket, these concepts may reveal more than Brain's sense of self importance. They may also reveal more than a crude iconoclasm in that they point to a brutal understanding of how to 'teach and lead' which Brain was to develop in the coming years.

Their first secular concert was at *The Limit* club in 1981. But their professionalism and credibility was most notably demonstrated in a benefit concert for the Lead Mill arts centre in which they supported The Fall and Cabaret Voltaire. They also played alongside a nascent U2 at Greenbelt Festival, weeks after U2's first single was released. They were offered the support slot on a national tour with U2 but turned it down because U2 were too overtly associated with Christianity. Jon Ingham says: 'We didn't want to have the Christian tag, we were trying to get rid of it.'

At this point Brain said that God had told him that the band was to stop playing live dates. They were to concentrate on writing new songs, rehearsing, working on image and producing an alternative avant-garde show. Another prophetic vision for the band started to emerge. It was based on the Old Testament Exodus story of the children of Israel leaving Egypt and entering the Promised Land. They were to live out the narrative in an allegorical fashion in which the stifling church culture was seen as Egypt and the Promised Land was club culture and the music industry which they were to reclaim for God. Brain, as the prophetic spiritual leader was seen as Moses and John Ingham, who as well as managing the band was acting as Brain's spokesperson, was seen as Aaron. 'My job was to make contact with outsiders, to establish a rapport with them, before introducing them to Chris, who wasn't good with people on first meetings', says Ingham.

As they sought to live out the biblical narrative, people associated with the band were sent as 'spies' into enemy territory to see how the enemy operated. That is, they went into clubs or concerts and reported back on what they had learned. The period in which the band were told to stop playing was called the 'wilderness years' and they shared their frustration as they waited for God to tell them when they should 'cross the river'. They were thorough in their preparations, researching cultural trends and the internal workings of the music industry. The inheritances, gifts and finances which were given to the project were seen as manna given by God. Just as the Israelites had to consume all the manna as an act of trust in God to supply their needs in the future, so the band had to spend all the money without saving any for the future. They saw no contradiction with their anti-consumption and simple lifestyle values. Neither did they see the potentially dangerous dualism of their approach to the outside world, which they saw as the enemy in dire need of their redemptive influence for Christ.

Perhaps, more significantly, this dualistic 'us and them', 'saved and unsaved' approach was the platform for their increasingly grand and wide ranging attacks on secular 'worldly values' of consumerism, greed, waste, lust, fame and power. The more fervent and idealistic their attacks on worldly values, the more insular, close-knit and defensive they became. Ingham recalls: 'We had a very strong identity as a community, there was us and there was everybody else, and they were all middle class people who were fudging the gospel.' They were still on a 'mission from God' but they were becoming increasingly cut off from the church as well as the outside world. As Brain said to me years later: 'We are on a dual exodus from church and from the values of modern society.' With the prophet and his lieutenants in place, a 'total vision', and a clearly shared ethos and culture, they had several cult-like characteristics which were to develop more fully as the vision unfolded.

By this time, they had set up the Nairn Street Community as a way of realising their vision. This was based on the call to a simple lifestyle by radical evangelical leaders like David Watson, Ronald Sider (author of *Rich Christians in an Age of Hunger*) and Jim Punton, leader of the Frontier Youth Trust. The community of about 30 lived together in houses (one of which was on Nairn St, adjacent to St Thomas's) in Crookes, shared their incomes and had weekly community meetings where they read the bible, prayed and discussed politics, culture and any issues that had come up for community members. They became a recognised fellowship group within St Thomas's with Brain as overall leader, Steve Williams, a former youth worker at St Thomas's, later to become pastoral leader, and Ingham as 'practical' leader or manager.

The Nairn Street policy document states: 'There should be genuine submission to the authority of the leaders.' It adds: 'Fellowship should be led by the Lord, not by personalities. The leaders need to recognise when people need leading as adults and when as children.' The leadership style was to 'sell decisions and bring in the opinion of others.' But Brain was the ultimate leader: 'Chris is the chairman of the leadership team, and therefore has veto; but the attitude should be that the leaders are subject to one another.'

Members of the community were committed to living on 'what was enough' and donating the surplus to a 'common purse'. The Nairn Street policy document states: 'There should be a central authoritative committee to corporately judge the needs of individual cases and make decisions (Steve, Jon and Chris).' Once what was enough had been ascertained the policy document says: '*All* money is to be given.' It also says: 'There should be a central community account, to be controlled at the leaders' discretion.' This common purse freed half the community from having to work, and enabled them to pursue the vision of radical Christianity and social justice single-mindedly. Strangely, it was only those closely involved with the band who were made aware of the importance of the band's centrality to the vision and the amount of time, money and energy that was being put into it. The financial system was flexible, but involved detailed budgeting of outgoings for clothes, food, and socialising before working out the donation to the common purse. The social money for individuals was £3.00 a week. Cheques were distributed to community members who were released to work on the band and on running the community.

It was this idealistic commitment to the disadvantaged that attracted Alan Gibson, a middle aged careers advisor, and his wife to join the Nairn Street Community in the early 1980s. He was fed up with what he saw as the shallow triumphalistic theology and low profile of justice issues at St Thomas's. 'We joined because we wanted a faith that expressed itself realistically in working to help the poor and by living simply as a rejection of the irresponsible consumer values of Western society', Gibson says. The Gibsons went into the community, giving approximately £500 per month. In the early years it appeared to embody values that the Gibsons felt were worthwhile. Poorer members of the community were supported and cared for, and some members were working to help those outside the community.

However, according to Gibson, gradually the centre of focus seemed to shift away from helping people. This came to a head when a message from Brain and the community leaders stipulated that each community household must be self-financing. 'This seemed to go against our ethics. Surely we were there to support each other within the community and this severely restricted this', he says. Later, when the Nine O'Clock Service started, he felt too much money and time were spent on the worship at the expense of serving others. 'We seemed to have lost our raison d'être, the community was completely wrapped up in researching, designing, and staging the service', he recalls.

As things progressed and the commitment to social justice became even less of a priority, Gibson was constantly placated with promises of future action as well as being given research projects on political action and the poor to carry out. He took these seriously but they were rarely acted upon satisfactorily. Nevertheless, the community was committed to a left-of-centre agenda, whilst the inner core was committed to the band which they believed would unveil this idealistic agenda to the secular public. They believed that the band was going to reach a national standing and have significant impact on the country. The Nairn Street policy document says: 'The band should be the Word of God to the world', adding: 'The band's ministry is to establish the Lordship of Christ over the Godless desert of rock music and its culture.' The method was a 'policy of attack and conquering'. For those involved with *Tense* the gritty idealism of justice issues and the glitzy world of the band were wrapped up in each other, but clearly there was a tension between the two.

However, whilst Gibson and others were living simply and donating large amounts of money to the community, Brain was receiving preferential treatment. He appeared incredibly busy and active in various projects and was given gifts of money, equipment and even a car. The Nairn Street policy document includes details of two 'fellowship cars'. One, an Austin Maxi, which was shared among the households (who all had a set of keys) and the other, a VW Polo, whose use was authorised by Brain who kept the keys. In addition to having his income paid by the community and receiving gifts, a PA hire company (Tense Productions) started by Jon

Ingham and Mark Estdale, made weekly donations to Brain as 'resource investigation expenses'.

This money, for things such as tickets to concerts, drinks and clothes, was paid for out of the so-called 'green tin' account. It was about five times as much as the social budget for most members of Nairn Street, but there were no complaints. This was partly because some people weren't aware of it but also because members occasionally benefited from it. Jon Ingham says: 'The thing is, if you went out with him you got your ticket paid for or your drinks bought.' He also points out that Brain was genuinely a brilliant resource investigator and that his job was to do the researching and thinking for the community. He was not just their prophet, he was their cutting edge visionary, constantly assimilating technical information for the band and cultural and theological information for the community.

Apart from going on anti-apartheid marches, working for social services and caring professions, there were other results following from their 'left-of-centre' world view. One was a suspicion of the nuclear family. It was seen as a conservative institution and the backbone of the Church, and in its sugary cereal packet format, seemed an affront to the community values that Nairn Street espoused. Because of this, and because couples without children could have more time to give to the community, heavy pressure was put on couples that joined not to have children. Couples that did were rejected by the rest of the community. Andy and Julie (not their real names) had been trying to have children for years, and unfortunately for them they succeeded whilst in the Nairn Street Community. Jon Ingham recalls: 'They got ostracised from the community for that.' He explains that the leadership decided that since they'd taken the decision to have children they would have to pay for it, and their financial support was not continued.

Andy explains that they had asked the Nairn Street leadership if they could have children and had been refused. The baby arrived at an awkward time soon after Andy lost his job and months after buying a new house. Nevertheless they were removed from the Nairn Street Community budget despite having contributed thousands to the community over a number of years. Andy recalls: 'It left us in an insecure position, but at the time we weren't angry.

Brain was such a powerful and enigmatic figure we accepted his decision.'

Another reaction against the nuclear family was what community members refer to as 'anti-couplism'. The culture within the community frowned on couples (whether married or not) spending time together. This was seen as going against the radical, sharing lifestyle that the community stood for. Indeed, it was seen as positively healthy for couples to accept their partners going out alone with members of the opposite sex. This was seen as a sign of healthy independence and trust. Ingham says of his relationship with his wife, 'We wouldn't be seen dead holding hands together, it was bad to be seen together at all.'

One member of Nairn Street describes how in bible studies in the early years, despite the apparent liberation from accepted norms, there were unwritten rules: 'People would lie around on bean bags and cushions, resting on other people's bodies; the only rule seemed to be that you were not to lean against your own married partner.' On one occasion he sat alone and watched as his wife lay down, placing her head in Brain's lap. Brain later confronted him about his reaction to this incident, telling him that he should release his wife from his possessiveness and his dominating, overbearing sexism.

If individuals felt vulnerable or jealous about their partners seeing members of the opposite sex, they were frequently told that they had a problem or that there was something in their marriage that needed sorting out. The stress on open relationships was such that the problem would usually be sorted out with the person who highlighted the problem rather than with the marriage partner. Not surprisingly this often compounded the problem, increased the jealousy and created a situation in which a person's confidante was often their friend of the opposite sex. People were discouraged from having their marriage partner as their confidantes.

Relationship boundaries were beginning to blur, and it was no surprise that rumours started circulating at St Thomas's about 'wife swapping' within the Nairn Street community. Indeed, when Sarah Collins was considering joining the community she confronted Brain about the rumours. She was told that there had been romantic and sexual improprieties, and Brain admitted that he had been involved in them and said that he was trying to put them behind him. At the time Sarah Collins was told there was a sort of sexual clampdown going on. She joined, attracted by their commitment to bring the gospel to the poor, and genuinely believing that this small idealistic nucleus had the potential to make a significant impact, even if they weren't going to turn the world upside down. Later she discovered that within weeks of their discussion Brain made unwelcome sexual advances to a member of the community.

Jon Ingham was also aware of Brain's sexual misdemeanours. He recalls: 'I knew that things had gone on and come to light and Chris would be in a state about it.' At the time he believed that Brain was struggling to conquer his weakness and he was assured that it wouldn't happen again. Ingham's view has changed: 'It always sounded as though he was genuinely struggling, it wasn't until the allegations ten years later that we realised the extent of it and that it wasn't the behaviour of someone that's genuinely struggling to change.'

One male member of the Nairn Street Community says that between 1982 and 1984 Brain was having an affair with his wife. He was unsettled about his wife arriving home from spending time with Brain in the early hours of the morning. Early one morning he confronted his wife and she admitted that she and Brain went to bed together on a regular basis. The member found out the details of what had been going on, which to his knowledge never involved full penetrative sex. 'The worst thing, after the initial shock, was that I was completely undermined as a person and my wife saw me through Brain's filter, and he, probably saw me as pathetic', he says. He wanted to leave NOS, but his wife refused and continued in a close relationship with Brain until NOS fell apart in 1995.

Simon Towlson, however, suggests that there may have been a genuine struggle within Brian concerning his sexual activity. He recalls an impromptu visit from Brain, whilst Towlson was studying in Bradford. The purpose of Brain's visit was to confess to his relationship with the singer in the band. 'He appeared genuinely upset about it and I'm sure that it was sincere, otherwise why travel all that way to volunteer the information,' Towlson says. 'We talked about it and prayed about it and he resolved to put it behind him,' he recalls. Towlson remembers Brain being full of remorse and saying that he was going to ask her to leave (she was living with them at the time). Shortly, afterwards she left.

By 1984 Brain said that God had told him that it was okay for the band (now known as *ICI*) to play again. The guitarist had left, frustrated at not playing and because of this they had started to experiment with samples and multi-track tape loops. Those close to the band had spent years sitting on the banks of the River Jordan and meticulous preparations were put into their first concert. In January 1985 *ICI* played at an out of town club, the Bradford *One in Twelve Club*. Half the community was completely wrapped up in the performance and the other half was ignored and kept in the dark. Many only found out about it a year later. *ICI* played a stunning set and were seemingly all set to make it big and take on the music industry. Ingham recalls with some embarrassment: 'Those that were full time were the artistic elite and those that had jobs were seen as being there to run the community and to service our needs to fulfil the mission.'

Meanwhile, the Nairn Street Community was about to be superseded by a larger vision. The community, however, was showing the genesis of several damaging characteristics, which were to prove the undoing of the ultimate experiment, the Nine O'Clock Service. The Nairn Street Community leadership structure, which was supposedly based on a democratic community, was in fact centred round Brain: a powerful, dominant and charismatic personality, who was seen by many as a prophet. The much talked about openness and equality was obscuring a community of secrecy and privilege. The ideal of open and free relationships was leading to closed and painful relationships. The rejection of Western consumerism was masking a fascination with high-tech equipment, fashion and other luxuries. Criticism of society's media-led obsession with glamour and fame seemed to mask a deeper desire for recognition and adulation.

Indeed, many would say that these paradoxes were all features of their charismatic, forceful and plausible leader. Rather than wrestle with these demons, they would say, he projected them on to the community (projection itself later became an issue) without resolving them. Whether or not this is correct, members of the community ignored or overlooked these contradictions and remained loyal to the vision for a number of different reasons. For some it may have been the feeling of importance of being ground breaking pioneers who were going to change the world, which blinded them to the truth. Others internalised the contradictions as their own problems.

The altruistic and radical vision of helping the disadvantaged clearly persuaded others to suspend their doubts. The intense and personal conversion experience of the evangelicals (which most of them were) added another serious reason for them to hold to the vision as the most vibrant part of their faith. Nearly all were overawed by their exceptionally gifted and dynamic leader, and his insight, determination and vision. He was seen as truly a modern Moses or John the Baptist; a latter-day prophet.

2

The Arrival of the Nine O'Clock Service

In 1985, John Wimber came to Sheffield. Wimber was a west coast American with a disarmingly affable temperament and an explosive theology. An ex-musician, Wimber had led a grassroots charismatic revival through his Vineyard churches throughout the United States. He was friends with British charismatics like David Watson and St Thomas's vicar, the Revd Robert Warren. His theology was, in essence, what he believed was a return to New Testament practices, with a very strong emphasis on practising the charismatic gifts such as healing people by the laying on of hands, prophecy and speaking in tongues. He encouraged all Christians to be involved in healing, receiving words of knowledge and speaking in tongues. He also taught the importance of exorcism (which he called deliverance) and saw Christians as engaged in a battle with demons and dark powers in the spiritual realm, in what he called spiritual warfare. Wimber's teaching was called 'signs and wonders' teaching, the idea being that as non-Christians saw these signs and wonders they would come to faith. He wrote books making grand claims about the power that Christians had through the Holy Spirit to heal and evangelise and prophesied that many of the cancer sufferers that he prayed for would be healed.

Wimber came to Sheffield City Hall and Robert Warren persuaded Chris and members of the Nairn Street fellowship to attend his meetings. He relates: 'It was not easy to get them to hear John Wimber when he came to speak at the Signs and Wonders conference; "Not another rich American selling triumphalism" was their attitude. But they came.' Many were dynamically affected at the meeting. Warren tells how Steve Williams (a key Nairn Street leader who was to become head of NOS's pastoral department) responded: 'He was in the middle of a cynical remark about the "hyping" of the atmosphere when the Holy Spirit came in such power on him that he slumped in his seat and experienced God taking him in the Spirit into another room and telling him that now things were to be done God's way.' From then on Warren had difficulty stopping them attending and bringing their friends along. According to Jon Ingham, at one of the follow-up meetings the 'whole community got blasted' and he stood crying, feeling both pain and compassion for the lost. Everyone was affected but Brain, although impressed, stood aloof.

'The anointing had come on us, and the community was absolutely transformed', Ingham recalls. The Nairn Street Community experienced a cleansing and purification process as they believed the Holy Spirit exposed various private sins, including bad attitudes, kleptomania and infidelity. It was a time of listening to God, of praying for healing, of exorcism and of what they saw as deep bonding through the Holy Spirit. Brain took these powerful spiritual methods on board and was soon exercising 'words of knowledge' about people, prophesying, practising healing and speaking in tongues. 'At the time we thought that he must have been holy to have this power, for God to have been using him like this', Ingham recalls, adding: 'I now see him as a man with tremendous spiritual insight and psychic power, who made good use of his abilities for his own ends and resisted allowing the searchlight to rest on him.' The community had been given new weapons to fight their war, to invade the Promised Land, and they were intoxicated with the power and the beauty of the weapons.

It was during the Wimber team's follow-up visit that Robert Warren believes he had a 'prophecy' concerning the Nairn Street Community. He says: 'In one of those rare moments that I know God has spoken to me, the thought "God wants to add 200 people like these to the church in the near future" was put in my head without my having put it there.' Warren realised that St Thomas's guitar strumming charismatic services weren't going to do the job and after much wrangling with the St Thomas's staff team and key members of the Nairn Street Community, it was decided that Brain and the Nairn Street Community would put on a service at nine o'clock each Sunday evening for a trial period of a year. The report for the St Thomas's Church Council stated the main aim was 'to provide a style of public worship which will help to provide an understanding and practice of orthodox Christianity amongst unchurched young people of a target audience age of 18-30.'

This was seen as an end to the wilderness years and a time when the community started to use their technological and musical knowledge to 'occupy the land' — although the land had shifted from the music industry to youth culture. The whole community put itself into this experimental service and members went into overdrive: writing music; designing the environment using lighting and wall-size slide projections; and working on rewriting the liturgy (and other 'Godwords') into a language that the target audience of young clubbers could understand. Despite the fact that the church was designed to resemble a night-club they used Wimber's service format of worship and teaching, then calling down the Holy Spirit as a model. As the Church Council report says: '[we intend to] use secular standards and concepts as reference, whilst redeeming the content.' It was to be a mixture of clubland cultural *nous* and Wimber's teaching. Stylistically, the avant-garde *ICI* musicians had to step back several years to create more positive music to appease the conservative outlook of St Thomas's. Without selling out they created a multi-media music based performance which managed to avoid the turgid, insipid or twee whilst clearly being heart stopping worship of a sort that had never been seen before.

It was a big success and within a year they had trebled in size with a regular congregation of about 150. As an example of mission it appeared to be working in a quite phenomenal way. However, although many unchurched people became Christians and joined, the growth was equally due to disillusioned young evangelicals hearing about the service and finding a context to worship in that was real to them, that reflected their lives rather than an archaic tradition or tub thumping, tambourine bashing triumphalism. Young people who had felt confined by the dogmatism and cultural alienation of evangelical and charismatic churches found a more open approach. They also found a congregation which clearly had social justice issues on their agenda — although they never quite got round to working with the poor in a structured, church based strategy.

A couple of years into the experiment, Brain and the leaders decided to completely overhaul the service. This was largely to meet differing needs in the membership. It was decided to design two different types of service, a communion and a teaching service. The communion service was more meditative and took pains to emphasise the symbolism of the sacraments. Brain was keen to react against the predominant reason-based approach to faith which he thought had come with the Reformation and the Enlightenment.

He thought this made Protestants, and particularly evangelicals and charismatics, too matey with God. He wanted to stress the 'otherness' of God, the distance between humans and God, the mystery of the creator rather than the quantifiable, reason-based perceptions which were derived from a wholly rational, post-Enlightenment world view. 'We want to discover the great treasures of pre-Reformation rituals', he said, adding, with the quiet iconoclasm of a man who doesn't underrate his own significance: 'We make everyone uptight, we're not just pre-Reformation, we're post-Reformation, we are going for very high symbolism.' With this in mind, Brain and the design team created a powerful, almost eerie, service.

The teaching service was much more exuberant. This was based on high octane, celebratory dance music. During worship the congregation stabbed the air and blew whistles as projections and film loops of scudding clouds, germinating seeds, cascades of water and crowds of shoppers, swept across the white walls of the nave. The teaching was supported by image based narratives projected on to the walls, highlighting the speaker's message or bringing out pertinent ironies or juxtapositions. Brain had been reading a number of postmodern texts and was keen that NOS should be at the cutting edge of cultural trends. He was aware that society was moving from a text based outlook to an image based one and wanted images to convey the message as much as the speaker's words. The service ended with more pulsating, invigorating dance music.

Brain was reading postmodern texts soon after they were published and, indeed, postmodernism was to have a significant effect on NOS. Postmodernism divides human civilisation into three phases, the ancient, the modern and the postmodern and suggests that between the First World War and the present a fundamental shift in human understanding has taken place. The ancient world was characterised by superstition, myth and mysticism which was superseded in the eighteenth century by a modernist world view based on a belief in reason, science and progress. This approach placed the human being (rather than a revered God) and his perceptions at the centre of the universe and incorporated a belief in man's ability to improve the world, to find solutions to problems (scientific or ethical). It was in essence a mechanistic, reason (and text) based approach — it reflected the possibility of reason improving the world with coherent explanations (known as meta-narratives) based in ethics and science.

Perhaps owing to the carnage of the First World War, Hiroshima, the environmental crisis or the multiplicity of differing voices that the media present, postmodernists no longer believe in progress or science or any absolute explanation of (or solution to) the human condition. They replace a mechanistic approach with a biological or holistic one, they move from reason to intuition (which includes mysticism and ritual), from text to image, from depth (based in ethical absolutes) to surface and style. Because there is no objective belief, nothing is to be taken seriously; everything is to be seen 'playfully', with irony. Artistically, there are no great principles, rather a 'white noise' of electronic communications and a pick-and-mix collage of styles, without analysis or definition. Blurring boundaries is central to the subjective postmodern situation.

Not only was NOS's use of image based multi-media effects and dance samples truly postmodern, but their emphasis on style and design and their attempts to communicate intuitively using visual and dramatic rituals, rather than reason-based texts, also reflected a postmodern view. Later their exploration and synthesis of a variety of Christian theologies (and also subsequently other faiths) was another expression of postmodernism. Their interest in sexual roles and boundaries, in new science and the environmental crisis, in reinventing pre-modern rituals with technology, also owes much to a postmodern understanding. Postmodernism was a significant subtext running through NOS's development.

At this stage many of the elements of Jon Ingham's prophetic vision appeared to be coming true. NOS services had massive projections, a band on the right in the darkness, the layout resembled a theatre. In addition Ingham, as manager and Brain's personal assistant, was at the back of the auditorium, and his mother joined the church, as in his vision. All that was missing was the performance art of City gents in the treadmill and the touring of the country that was part of his picture. The vision wasn't yet fulfilled.

By 1988 there were 400 members, with dishevelled, black clad alternative looking youths queuing down the street to enter. However, the church authorities really started to take notice when in 1989, David Lunn, Bishop of Sheffield, confirmed nearly one hundred people. They were thrilled by the growth in numbers among these young people that the church had thus far failed to reach. Robert Warren recalls that the establishment started to sit up and listen: 'It was clear that something major was going on. Thus far we'd had no success in reaching street culture with the Christian message.' The NOS leaders prepared meticulously for the event with sound checks, slide checks, rehearsals and even having customised black cassocks made.

Sarah Collins, who was a member of the leadership team, was asked to lead the worship partly because the leaders knew that David Lunn was opposed to women priests, and because they wanted to endorse women in leadership. She had some experience at leading from the front and teaching, and when preparing her first sermon a year or so earlier had been asked by Brain to read it in front of him and two other leaders. She'd agreed to do this, understanding that it would help prepare her for the real thing. However, when she started the leaders went into caricature roles. One acted continually distracted, she says, the other pretended to be bored and was almost falling asleep. Brain sat opposite her, looking at her lecherously with his tongue hanging out. After about five minutes Sarah was in tears and Brain then explained that it was a way of preparing her for the worst.

At the confirmation service, the worst came true. Sarah was sitting nervously in her black cassock, cue cards in hand, with Brain and another leader sitting on the stage beside her. Moments before she was ready to step up to speak, she says, Brain whispered in her ear asking her what she was wearing underneath her cassock. She went to the front, spoke and sat down. Again, seconds before she was to make her next contribution, Brain leaned towards her and whispered about what he'd like to do to her underneath her cassock. He continued whispering disconcerting suggestions to her throughout the service. Sarah maintained her composure and carried out her responsibilities. At the end of the service, she confronted him about what he'd been doing and, with the confidence of a man who knows his authority and influence, he passed it off as a joke. She never mentioned it again, to Brain or anybody else, until the allegations against Brain came out in August 1995.

In spring, 1989 there were other instances of abusive behaviour towards his leaders. On April 15th the whole of Sheffield was traumatised by the Hillsborough disaster in which nearly a hundred football fans were crushed to death after crowds of spectators poured into an enclosure that was already full. Sarah Collins was watching events on the television and she phoned Brain to say that she was going down to see if she could offer any help to the emergency services. She arrived and was enlisted to take the relatives of Liverpool fans into a room with the walls covered with pictures of scores of corpses, some crushed so badly that they were unrecognisable. There were hundreds of relatives desperate to find out if members of their families were dead or in hospital. Sarah saw that the emergency services (including scores of clergy that the Sheffield Diocese had organised) were struggling to cope and phoned Brain asking for more people to come and help, particularly requesting NOS members who would be able to relate to football fans and their families. Six others came down.

They worked through the night, comforting distressed relatives, taking them into the photo room and then into the room in which the corpses were laid out for them to identify their relatives. At 4am, she was with the parents of a fourteen year-old trying to find their son without any success. Someone said that they thought he was in the hospital and the three of them were about to set off when they were stopped and taken to a mangled body at the end of the room. It was the missing son. Sarah tried to comfort the parents, crying but feeling numbed by the night's events. She went home and collapsed in bed at 6am. An hour later Brain arrived and asked her partner if he could see Sarah. He agreed but said she was asleep upstairs. Brain went upstairs and climbed into bed with her and started stroking her hair. She came round and Brain continued stroking her hair, telling her how proud he was of her for what she had done. Sarah, exhausted, soon went back to sleep.

That night NOS had planned a service in a Sheffield night-club called *Fruit*. They decided to go ahead and, according to many involved, in the midst of the pain and trauma of Hillsborough the worship was deeply moving. Sarah recalls a lot of silence and prayer for the bereaved families and throwing herself into the worship and experiencing total suffering but also a transcendent joy and sense of overcoming the horror. Julian Shinn, a young social worker, had also helped at Hillsborough and remembers

Brain coming up to him at the *Fruit*, during the service, and hugging him. 'I wept and wept, I was distraught at what I'd seen', he remembers.

The next day Brain flew to California to stay with John Wimber. During his stay Brain met Wimber's friends, a somewhat maverick group known as the Kansas City Prophets. Brain later told the leaders that one of the prophets had a 'prophetic picture' of Brain surrounded by evil in the form of hornets flying in a swarm round his head. Then a sword came down from heaven and chopped off his head. On his return to Sheffield Brain brought the leadership team together and told them of the vision. He then went on to attack them saying that they were the evil hornets surrounding him. He shouted and screamed at them, accusing them of conspiring against him, telling them that their evil was threatening the whole venture because God's avenging sword was poised to come down and destroy the vision.

He said that they had to sort themselves out or leave the church and that if they did this they would face divine wrath and lose God's protection. The leaders, who weren't unused to being accused of conspiracy against Brain, were nevertheless stunned. This was a serious ultimatum. They were being accused of evil; they must, therefore, be evil. They had no idea of what they had done wrong; the very idea of conspiring against Chris in his absence was unthinkable. They wouldn't think (or dare) to criticise him to each other. Citing the possibility of losing God's protection was, in effect, placing a divine death threat over their heads. The effect of Brain's attack was to encourage guilt and fear, not counterattack. What *could* they be doing that was so undermining their world-changing vision?

However, Brain reserved a special accusation for Sarah Collins. He took her aside and told her that her behaviour at Hillsborough had been evil. She had been operating in the egoistic, self reliant, 'fleshly' mode, he said. Her work at Hillsborough had been one massive act of vanity and he never wanted her to mention it again or to use the trauma of it as an excuse for 'out of order' behaviour. Sarah left the meeting completely disorientated and, with the threat of losing God's protection, frightened of being killed in a freak accident. She never mentioned Hillsborough again but, as if to rub salt in the wound, two weeks later at a conference in Leeds on the Church and social action, Brain got up and announced that NOS were so respected in the community for their social action that the council authorities had approached them for help during the Hillsborough disaster. According to Brain's version of events, NOS's involvement had nothing to do with Sarah Collins's compassionate response to watching the television coverage of the disaster.

So why did the leaders allow these malign outbursts, mind games and abuses of power to go on? Initially the Nine O'Clock Service leaders were members of the Nairn Street Community and many of them were already under his influence and had known and looked up to him for years. They considered him a brilliantly creative artist and leader, a radical visionary and a prophet. The whole culture of the inner core was based round respect for Brain. To oppose him meant facing not only Brain's considerable temper but being ostracised by the rest of the leadership team. He was a remarkably quick thinker and a very strong personality who didn't suffer fools (or dissidents) gladly. Many of them, thinking that they had a special relationship with him, had shared their vulnerabilities with him on a deep and intimate level. Most thought that he had divinely given insights and gifts.

It is also true that during the early years Brain was a good friend to many of the leaders and others in NOS. Many say that he was much more approachable and more human at this stage. Steve Williams says: 'Brain's enthusiasm, motivation, his vision and his intellect were attractive to all sorts of people and in the first two years he made some wise, good and generous decisions.' He adds: 'From 1988 onwards his need for control was all consuming; it consumed himself and the nice bits of himself.' Williams believes that it was Brain's choices and his personality defects which led to a deterioration in his behaviour: 'He's not a demon. He became an increasingly evil man who progressively lost contact with his conscience and his humanity.' In addition Brain's 'vision' was truly attractive and radical. Many of his views about the Church and society were incredibly pertinent. Western consumerism, the divide between rich and poor, first world and Third World, sexism, racism, all these things needed confronting and challenging and they were issues that the Church and society at that time, were often avoiding. Brain also railed against a media-led culture based around 'image', soundbite and glitz. He was critical of a theology based solely on reason and not including mystery or the mystical. Brain's agenda was, they thought, the right one and he was, apparently, a trailblazer, not writing books about it, but actually doing it. He was a world first.

Steve Williams points out that Brain recruited gifted leaders with different talents from all walks of life with one vital ingredient: an awareness of their faults and weaknesses. He says: 'They needed to be the sort of people who were initially self confident and capable but who were also aware of their own failings, who were trusting and committed, those to whom it was easy to suggest more failings and who gradually would abdicate their morality, intellect and relationships to this higher and more capable being.'

Thus Williams would spend days writing and rewriting sermons and scripts for leading services and Brain would arrive at the rehearsal and tear them to shreds and Williams would accept it. Once when Williams was reading his script during a rehearsal Brain took the microphone, told Williams that it was 'f---ing crap' and that he was a liar for saying that he had worked on it for 15 hours. Brain turned to the 20 or so present and said: 'You see, ladies and gentlemen, Steve thinks he has so much experience that he doesn't need to work like you all have to. He doesn't have to because his father's a vicar, and he knows everything about God and the Church. Well, I have news for you, it's bullshit.' He then turned to Williams and told him to get out of his sight, saying that he would deal with him later and asked another leader to take over. In another rehearsal Brain took the microphone and told him that he was walking round 'like a poof in that cassock', snatched his notes and mimicked him for several minutes. Everybody laughed.

This laughter is evidence of Williams' second point on Brain's controlling techniques. Once he had elicited the uncritical support of leaders, he had to periodically isolate them from others in leadership to maintain their loyalty. Williams says Brain was careful to isolate potential trouble makers by warning others away from them, and by suggesting that it would be bad for their spiritual growth to associate with them. 'Brain was paranoid about this and was so controlling; he could easily poison minds against a person, as and when he chose', Williams says. He adds: 'People were told who they could or could not go on holiday with, who single people could go out with, who people should marry and who they should break off engagements with, using the argument of protecting people from other damaging people.'

Williams believes that only those who had been promoted to the inner circle could be aware of Brain's inconsistencies, but by that time they were so aware of their own faults, so committed to the NOS vision and so enthralled by Brain that standing up to him became an impossibility. 'The closer you got to the centre the more pieces of the jigsaw you faced. At the same time, the closer in you were, the less you wanted to put the pieces of the jigsaw together and face the challenge of what to do about it', he says.

Yet in many ways Brain genuinely was at the 'cutting edge' in his thinking. He had an insatiable appetite for reading books about theology, philosophy, culture and the arts. As NOS thrived and got wider recognition, it was also clear that the experiment was a resounding success. It worked. Hundreds were coming to faith, giving money and joining the church. The service as well as the theological agenda was a massive and dramatic affirmation of the vision. Each service in itself was a strong statement of vision and otherness, uniqueness and possibly, brilliance. Their fame spread so fast that scores of clergy and church workers started visiting. At one service Brain delivered a stinging attack on the visitors, telling them in no uncertain terms that NOS was a community and not an entertainment for 'viewers'. They were not welcome. The dramatic success was a definite factor in the leaders suspending their judgement of Brain and his behaviour. If he was so right in so many areas, probably he was right in the areas that they were less happy with. Probably the problem lay with them.

Possibly because the leaders accepted Brain's behaviour so readily, some of them started to copy his methods with congregation members under their authority. Jon Ingham, who had burnt his mementoes and photos of his 'old life' as a sign of his commitment to the NOS vision, made similar demands on Julian Shinn. 'Jon told me that keeping my old friends was a sign of my lack of commitment to NOS. He wanted me to drop them', Shinn says. It was assumed by congregation members that total commitment was needed and such confrontations were commonplace.

Elizabeth (not her real name), who as a staff member had given up her 'old life' and made considerable financial contributions to NOS, asked Paul Hatton out for a meal to discuss his 'giving' to

NOS. 'It wasn't abusive in a direct way but very subtly it was suggested that my commitment was lacking, that I had an extravagant lifestyle and that I should give more', he says. Elizabeth noted that Hatton was wearing a tie from a professional association. 'I feel there was an agenda behind that observation. It was being suggested that I was committed to my profession rather than the church. It was innocuous but the subtext was loud and clear', he adds. If total commitment was demanded of the leaders by Brain, this was passed on to members in a gentler (but still manipulative and controlling) way. Hatton claims that there was one leader whose main job was to confront people over their lack of commitment.

The leaders, staff members and key people were all, at this stage, almost completely uncritical of Brain. Although as individuals, they may have had greater musical or artistic ability, intelligence or managing skills, no one knew how to read people as well as he could, and no one could bring it altogether with such 'front' and commitment. He was the dynamo, he orchestrated the whole, and his leaders and staff revered him. Brain also had a sharp, biting wit. He was a master at belittling people or simply deriding them. The leaders were, no doubt, keen to avoid being on the receiving end and silence and affirmation were the surest way of doing this. He was not only a visionary, he was drop-dead cool, and it was only too easy to look stupid in front of him.

3

Welcome to NOS, a New Reality

New members could have no idea of the abuses and behaviour within the inner core. All they saw was a radical, challenging and vibrant form of Christianity. It was a place where they could be themselves, a place that they often thought they had been looking for. Twenty-something Mel Lloyd was visiting Sheffield and remembers her first visit to NOS as a life-changing one: 'It was fantastic. Graham Cray, a vicar from St Michael-le-Belfrey, York, was teaching about the importance of social action and the church was full of really down to earth but trendy people, they were all dressed in black.' A month later she became a Christian and shortly after she joined the church membership. Julian Shinn's introduction was whilst studying to become a social worker at Sheffield University. He was also impressed by what he saw: 'It was a service like nothing on earth, it was everything that I could have hoped for, genuine worship and fellowship, music that you could actually put all of yourself into whilst worshipping, then times of silence, meditating and listening to God.'

Carol (not her real name) who had a background in the conservative-minded charismatic, house church movement was also deeply affected: 'It was just like coming home.' She says: 'It was so passionate, it was idealistic about issues that I could relate to, the worship had hard hitting images, pumping bass lines, I could relax and let myself go.' Her younger sister, who first attended when she was 15, agrees: 'It was incredible. I loved the music, I experienced God, it was a dream come true and the people were real, normal people, not the usual church types. They accepted and valued me for who I was.' Once again disillusioned evangelicals and charismatics were buying into a vision and the Nine O'Clock Service breathed new life into their increasingly frustrating, narrow minded faith and the converts were hooked. After the Nine O'Clock Service where else was there for them to go?

But behind the powerful, emotive projections, the 'in your face' music and the easy going but carefully manicured leadership style, all was not as it seemed. Brain had, by charisma, insight, determination and his forceful personality created a leadership structure which was almost completely dominated by him. He had surrounded himself with leaders who were in awe of him and the passion and creativity that he brought to his vision. Many of the members of *ICI* who were placed in positions of authority already recognised him as the leader and the main creative force, and the Nairn Street Community considered him the radical visionary behind the community. Most of them considered Brain to be prophetic.

New members of the congregation were soon completely in awe of him. This was partly because of the extreme reverence with which he was treated by the inner core. This fantastic ground breaking church, that produced such phenomenal multi-media worship and had such a socially radical agenda was always spoken of as the 'vision' of this mysterious, cool and distant character. The leadership team conferred on Brain such mystique, vision and charisma that it was soon picked up by new members. He was always surrounded by a group of admiring people, and he painstakingly maintained his distance from others until they were sufficiently in awe of him to make a meeting (or confrontation) seem a privilege or honour. Newcomers couldn't go up to Brain for a chat or to ask about the service. Everything about the service, the culture and his hip entourage conferred status: this was an important and enigmatic man, he was the man who would change things

Some outsiders may have thought that he was self important and vain, but if they did they generally wouldn't return to the service. But Christians who had become disillusioned with their faith or 'unchurched' people who were seeking, had never seen anything like it and they wanted to belong. For these people the power relationship was never on an equal footing. They were only ever going to get to know Brain on his terms and he made sure that he made them wait. The service and his doting (but remarkably able and articulate) entourage created an incredible aura around him. And at the heart of this service were positive, life enhancing ideals about the poor, justice, and community. The sort of things that many were eager to be a part of, but which in a depersonalised society they felt helpless to confront. As a community, and a community in an intense but fulfilling spiritual relationship which appeared to nourish them, people felt that they could make a difference.

When Brain was ready to start a relationship, with a view to inviting someone into deeper involvement in NOS, he used certain techniques to make sure that he was in control. His initial approach was often compassionate, humble and affirming. But his uncanny insight into people's weaknesses and vulnerabilities soon became a key factor. When he was confident that someone was sufficiently in awe of him, he would confront them with a perceived weakness, usually subtly but sometimes in a more direct way. Once taking on the role of prophet, he stood directly in front of a person, pointing at them between the eyes and telling them with an air of total authority, what their weakness was. Usually his perceptions were right, and if they weren't, his influence was such that they would accept his insight and think that they themselves hadn't realised it.

This sort of practice wasn't seen as intrusive or abusive but as a sign of Brain's commitment to the person. This kind of radical discipleship was seen as necessary because of the totality of the 'vision'. The weaknesses that Brain highlighted weren't always personal, they were often an apparent, surface feature about the person that made them feel somehow excluded from the vision. Middle class people were made to feel it. There was a sense that their backgrounds somehow excluded the values of the NOS community, that they were little rich kids and NOS was (supposedly) solidly working class. People with church backgrounds, or older people, were made to feel that they were impostors as they didn't fit into this authentic club culture experiment. People without education were made to feel inadequate in front of Brain's extensive knowledge of ground breaking theologians, management gurus or philosophers.

Fiona's (not her real name) experience was quite typical. Arriving in Sheffield in 1988, she joined what was then known as the NOS community and was soon giving most of her money to the NOS account in St Thomas's. An old friend of Brain's from Harrogate, initially she had a lot of access to the Brains and their house and Brain gave her a lot of pastoral input. During their sessions together, he asked her if she'd been sexually abused, if she was anorexic and told her that she was awkward in company and socially inadequate. Although she hadn't spoken about depression, he suggested that she'd recently been depressed. She was feeling lonely, vulnerable and emotionally unstable despite having found a good job as a hostel manager. Brain also started saying that to really be part of NOS, Fiona had to be 'of the culture' (a phrase which meant to be part of club culture). Fiona wanted to be fully involved and was keen to 'cross cultures', but to do so she needed Brain's agreement as well as help to chose a new set of clothes.

She'd seen Brain jeering at people behind their backs who were trying to look 'of the culture' and was wary of this happening to her if she went out shopping on her own. She didn't trust her judgement of club culture fashions. Another NOS member, Tony (not his real name), unofficially had the job of 'styling' people who wanted to 'cross cultures' and to do it properly she had to go shopping with him. Brain held out the possibility of crossing cultures as a carrot, but Fiona was made to wait nearly a year until it actually happened. Fiona says: 'In June 1989 he agreed that I could change culture and he sent me out shopping with the NOS stylist. For two days running I bought a lot of clothes and I asked if I could wear the clothes at the end of the expedition. I was told by Chris that if I wore them I could never wear the old clothes again.'

She agreed and put her old clothes into black bin liners, put her gear on and had someone come round to put appropriate club style make up on. She adds: 'He then got me to dye my hair and said: 'Hmm, you could perhaps do with losing a little bit of weight.' Fiona lost a stone and on her next visit home her family thought that she might have an eating disorder. There were other aspects to changing culture, indeed it was almost a form of baptism. The old life had to be dropped in its entirety and the new one embraced and explored. This involved leaving old pastimes behind and throwing oneself into the new lifestyle.

Thus Fiona stopped reading novels and knitting and started listening to dance music and clubbing. There was even a reading list which included John Wimber's *Power Healing* and David Watson's *Discipleship* as well as recommended trendy but sophisticated magazines like *The Face* and *ID*. It was called 'research'. From this point on 'black clad made-over' Fiona had little personal contact with Brain although she was wholly committed, and Tony the stylist told her that hers had been an 'easy transition', so it seemed much of it must have been innate. However, not surprisingly, Fiona felt somehow false, having reinvented herself in a weekend. Fiona explains: 'Although I integrated into club culture fairly well, at the back of my mind I was wondering about discarding my old life like that, and in some senses I felt an impostor.' At the end of crossing cultures Fiona's integrity appears to have been undermined and her dependence on NOS was reinforced.

'Chrisnapping' was another way that Brain got to know his membership. He would drive the streets in his car and invite a member to get in and go for a drive. He would explain that he was so busy in research, service design and running the church that this allowed him to get to know his church members quickly. The unsuspecting member was invariably intrigued by this enigmatic, forceful visionary who somehow encapsulated all that they loved about the service. They were flattered by his interest and attention. Driving the streets of Sheffield or into the Pennines he would then start throwing completely unexpected questions or statements at them. It was a game, he said, that allowed him to shortcut preliminaries and get to the essence of the person. Sometimes he'd ask them where they saw themselves in the NOS vision, and what they'd really like to do. Sometimes he'd spot a weakness and confront them with it. He would ask questions about their past, sometimes intimate details of former relationships. He would always cut to the core within minutes.

He would sometimes 'prophesy' things about the person. 'Prophecy' allowed him to say things without taking responsibility for them as they were, after all, supposedly words from God. If a music tape was playing he sometimes said he felt that there was a message in the song for them. He had a penchant for playing certain songs (including Seal's *Killer* with the refrain *Solitary Sister* and New Order's *Living in Sin*)and then saying: 'What a coincidence this song is playing, God must be speaking to you through it' as he persuaded them into opening themselves up on a deep level. On some occasions passengers had a chance to ask him questions. He would respond but, according to his passengers, never by opening himself up in a full and vulnerable way. He might speak about his philosophical or idealistic vision and the new directions that he thought it was taking. The names of theologians and modern philosophers would trip off his lips with complete aplomb. He might hint at their future involvement in exciting projects, projects which would take them closer to the inner core of the NOS machine, closer to the heart of this spinning, passionate vision. He left them either asking more questions or fascinated by this enigmatic prophet. When he dropped people off they were usually elated at receiving such intimate and personal contact and bewildered, but excited, by the meeting. Often it was taken as a portent of increasing involvement in the vision.

Sian, a PhD. scientist, joined NOS because she felt that it allowed her freedom to be her own person within a religious environment; it appeared to be a church structure which offered her the opportunity to find her own internal integrity. She was deeply impressed by the radical new form of Christianity and admits to being a 'naive idealist'. The life-giving rhetoric and the apparent desire to work with the disadvantaged drew her in. Sian's experience of Chrisnapping was revealing. One night in 1989 Brain drove up beside her as she was walking home, wound down his window, looked directly at her and opened the door. She got in and he explained that this was called Chrisnapping and that it was a way of getting to know people through questioning 'games' in which they each asked each other questions in turn.

She felt nervous, but saw it as a challenge. He asked her what it was like being married to Mark, what sort of ministry she'd like to be involved in, and what she'd most like to change about herself. Sian in turn asked Brain what he'd be doing if he weren't leading NOS. He answered: 'I think I'd be dead or in prison.' She asked him how he felt about things, but his answers were evasive and based around information rather than his feelings. She asked if he enjoyed being a leader and he replied that he didn't enjoy it. He said: 'You've always got to watch out for the three Gs.' Sian asked what he meant and he replied: 'Gold, glory, and girls.' Gold, he explained, meant that you couldn't go out for your own financial gain, glory meant that you couldn't build up your ego, while girls were difficult because they found men with power attractive.

For others, a Chrisnapping experience was more damaging. Carol was in her early twenties when she was first given a lift in Brain's car. Completely in awe of this leader that she had rarely spoken to, she was nervous but also flattered by his interest as he sowed the seeds of the relationship. Then after services he would come up to her, take her into a corner and tell her that he had a 'word of knowledge' (prophecy) for her and arrange to go for a drive afterwards to talk about it. During other drives Brain told her that she had low self esteem and that this would be the greatest problem in her life. She explains: 'He would say totally damning things and I'd feel angry because I totally believed him and I was upset that this was going to be a problem all my life.' He told her that she saw herself a totally plastic person and that her looks were all that she had and countered by saying he thought she was beautiful and that he didn't just mean physically. 'Then', Carol says, 'I'd feel totally loved and cared for and feel that here was a person that can see beyond this and love me for who I am and that was very enticing.'

He told Carol that she'd been very damaged by her past relationships. 'This was a bit like telling me that I was in a complete mess and then saying that he could help me', she said. Carol then started feeling that she had to know this man, that he was the answer to her problems. She fell in love with him and told him. Brain said that this often happened with women. At this point Carol says she was in the palm of his hand, feeling incredibly special and loved and that she could relate to him as she could with nobody else. Then, however, he would turn on her for no discernible reason and she was totally ignored. On one occasion, a fortnight after he recommended that Carol needed prayer for emotional healing, she asked him to pray for her after a service. Carol says: 'He turned on me and basically said what the f--- are you asking me to pray for you for?' She reminded him that he'd offered to pray with her earlier and he pointed to a prayer team, looked at her as though she were a complete fool and said: 'What's wrong with them?' Carol was devastated and completely confused by his change in behaviour but was nevertheless to be 'affirmed' in her relationship with Brain in more damaging ways as NOS progressed.

Leaders were also Chrisnapped. Steve Williams tells of receiving phone calls from Brain on his mobile phone in which Brain would tell him that he was waiting for him outside in his car. Williams was expected to drop everything and go for a ride. He says: 'Brain would drive around for hours at a time, going over something about you or some perspective that he wanted you to have on someone else, or on a theological issue or new idea, and you would not be let out of the car until you submitted or agreed with him.' Williams describes it as a 'lucky dip' because, sometimes the talks could be exciting and positive but his initial reaction was always fear. He adds: 'If he really wanted you to swallow something big he would bring someone else along to give weight to his views. But of course that person would have just gone through the same experience in the car, so they would back him up.'

These techniques weren't restricted to the car. Brain would 'prophesy' at the drop of a hat and his prophecies could be quite colourful. Within the first year of her joining, Brain had a 'prophecy' concerning one young woman. Brain had a picture of her in frilly knickers involved in very graphic acts with someone called Martin. Did it ring any bells? No. Was she sure that it didn't mean anything to her? Yes. Nevertheless, Brain continued describing his picture cum prophecy for half an hour. She says: 'It seems to me that Brain was confusing prophecy and fantasy.'

Another method he used to open people up was a personal disclosure board game called the Un Game. However, when Moira (not her real name) played with Brain it was a doctored version in which some of the questions focused on sex. Moira remembers playing and being asked what she fantasised about when she masturbated. She wouldn't answer and Brain became really angry. She was told that it was another example of her refusing intimacy with Brain, rejecting his friendship and showing a resistance to his leadership. Shortly afterwards she was dropped as a friend by Brain and relieved of her post in the pastoral department, despite the fact that months before she had given up a career to take on the post.

In effect after a 'power encounter' Brain had intimate knowledge of the hopes, fears and weaknesses of congregation members. They often had a warm glow, an increased respect and reverence for their leader and an expectation of being taken into the vision. Usually they wouldn't get a chance to speak to him again for months, or even years. He was masterful at 'working' people and getting inside their heads, but also at letting them drop, having them chafing at the bit and waiting for the invitation into the dynamic centre. But the member would have no sense of having been a recipient of what seems to have been a stage-managed abuse of power.

Many members speak of another similar controlling technique that Brain used. In essence, this involved finding out what their aspirations were and affirming them, involving them, flattering them and then, for no perceptible reason, either completely rejecting them in a very direct and unequivocal way or distancing himself from them and implying that they weren't yet ready to fulfil their calling. This sort of behaviour would usually happen with either a staff member or a person working in a key role in ministry, music, art or design. Brain may ask them out for meals, or to meet him for an interview or even invite them out to see a band. (People simply didn't say 'no' to Brain. Everything else was dropped for this rare and privileged encounter — to turn him down could result in being cold shouldered or put down by him publicly). Then, he would tell them how valued they were, what a vital contribution they could make, and how gifted they were. He would listen to them and compliment them. He might also unearth the individual's personal problems.

After flattering them, and making them eager to go forward, Brain would either totally ignore them, keep them on the periphery (occasionally implying that there was some inadequacy that was holding them back) or, if they were vulnerable enough, turn on them viciously and tear them to shreds. He was a master at non-verbal communication, frequently staring through people as though they didn't exist, or staring straight at them as if they didn't deserve to. He was also pretty good at verbal communication as many that were close to him testify. The recipient of such rejection rarely saw the behaviour as abusive. If they did, it was clear Brain had misjudged them, and he rarely did that. His timing and intuition were impeccable.

Indeed, this treatment appears to have become a matter of policy in some instances. Paul and Fiona Thomson were working independently on an "alternative worship" experiment in Aberdeen. Initially, Brain was excited that others were involved in the same area and they were welcomed as fellow travellers by NOS. According to Paul, NOS invited them down to Sheffield in July 1989, and gave them an extraordinarily warm welcome. He says: 'We were met at the station and taken to stay at the home of one of the wealthiest members of the congregation, we were given a gift of £100 and a tourist pack, and we were even given a member of the leadership team as a "holiday rep"'. Both the slick efficiency and the warmth of their reception mystified them and they said so.

Three years later the Thomsons were tired of leading the Aberdeen congregation, NOS affirmed their decision to join and promised they would be welcomed and involved. However, when they arrived they were largely ignored and given no responsibilities. Thomson says: 'We'd committed ourselves by moving and gradually it dawned on us that none of our old friends in the leadership wanted to know us; there seemed to be a policy of shunning us and I've since found out that people were told not to associate with us.' They asked leaders about why they had seen side-lined but never got a satisfactory explanation. Thomson says: 'It wasn't a matter of pride; it was simply that we were being socially shunned with no explanation. It could have been an attempt to humiliate or undermine us as people or it could have been an oversight.'

Other people who were given similar treatment lived in a sort of limbo. They were told that they were carrying problems that they had to sort out (sometimes specific, sometimes undefined), but were promised 'progress' once these issues had been dealt with. Some describe this as severe psychological abuse, others as causing unhealthy introversion and neuroses. If their frustrations got the better of them and they quarrelled with those in authority they were very quickly shunned by all except close friends. Some were labelled misogynist or autistic or competitive behind their backs. Occasionally they rebelled and left, but usually the sense of there being no other church that could accommodate such a radical and relevant vision stopped them. NOS left them constantly turned inward, asking themselves what they were doing wrong. Self questioning was a common factor in their dealings with Brain and other NOS pastoral leaders. Members were rarely clear about where they stood or what they should do and the questions produced an intense dependence, because they concerned the foundations of their personalities.

This dependence and commitment had major financial consequences for most members of NOS. Most members' contribution was a proportion of their salaries (which the finance department dealt with), but occasionally they gave large, 'one off' payments, in terms of property, savings or inheritances. Mark Estdale, one of Brain's early friends from Harrogate, tells how he was walking in the park with Brain one day when he told him of a £20,000 inheritance that he had recently received.

After talking about the importance of the NOS vision, Brain asked Estdale how much of the inheritance he was going to donate to NOS. Estdale said perhaps half of it. Brain's next words were: 'That's a measure of your commitment to NOS', and started persuading him to give more. Estdale stuck to his guns and gave £10,000. 'It sounds strange but the whole culture of NOS was extreme and total commitment was built into the fabric of our lives', he says. 'At the time I was happy to give. I was friends with Chris, he was a creative dynamo full of energy and I was committed to NOS', Estdale adds. Once Estdale made the donation, Brain had no further social contact with him.

Daniel (not his real name) was a leader on the Arts Team when his mother, his only living relative, died in 1990. The death had not been expected and Daniel was in shock. Having travelled across the country to sort out his mother's affairs he returned to Sheffield. The next morning Brain phoned and asked him out for a meal. However, this wasn't going to be an opportunity for a minister to offer sympathy or succour to a member of his congregation. According to Daniel, Brain's first words on sitting down at the table were: 'I'm not going to bullshit. What are you going to do with your inheritance?' He was speechless. Brain continued: 'I want to tell you what to do with your money: buy yourself a house; and one for another leader; get yourself a biscuit and give the rest to the church.' He gave Daniel a deadline of noon the next day by which time he expected a decision.

Daniel spoke to his wife and to friends. They were horrified and furious. Ten minutes after the noon deadline the next day Brain phoned and said: 'Why the f--- haven't you phoned me, I thought we had a deadline.' Daniel was called to the NOS offices but found Brain in the soundproof studio. He was furious, screaming at Daniel for breaking the agreement and not taking Brain's advice. Unfortunately for Brain, Daniel was in no mood for such treatment. 'I went mental', he says, 'I very nearly attacked him. I only just stopped myself.' Brain immediately softened (and never shouted at him again) but didn't forget about the money.

Brain then delegated the job of eliciting the money to the others in leadership. Daniel was so angry that he held on to the money for 18 months. During this time, others in the leadership ignored and sidelined him. Eventually a member of the leadership approached him and told him that his position as a NOS leader was untenable whilst he was sitting on so much capital, at which point he gave several thousand pounds. Daniel now says: 'Basically it was a veiled threat but at the time the NOS arts was the focus of my whole life. I'm not known for being malleable, but I was so deeply into NOS and the whole reality that surrounded it that it seemed the right thing to do.'

John Chambers is one congregation member who testifies to a more positive side to Brain's nature. Having joined years earlier and realised that he wasn't what the leadership team were looking for in terms of taking on responsibility, Chambers resided, with many others, relatively comfortably on the periphery of NOS. A rugged geologist who was frequently away working on oil rigs, he was concerned at the deference towards Brain shown by the whole congregation but particularly the leaders. 'There was this highly unhealthy idea that the ground he trod was sacred, and I thought that he must be very isolated. I decided it would be good to invite him out for a drink as a way of treating him as a normal human being, rather than a leader on a pedestal,' he says. He sent him a letter asking him out and weeks later a letter came from Brain saying that he'd really like to go out for a drink and it was good to receive such a positive letter and a secretary would be in touch to set up a meeting. 'I wanted to chat to him about normal things, to get to know him as a normal person, not a leader or visionary, and to chat to him in this way about the pressures of leading such a radical church,' Chambers says.

Six months later one of Brain's secretaries phoned Chambers saying that Brain may be free in the next few days but she couldn't say when . Chambers says, 'I wasn't going to change my timetable to fit in with the remote possibility of such a meeting. I had made an effort to break through the NOS bureaucracy that surrounded him: but going out for a drink seemed for whatever reason, too difficult'. He later received a call from one of Brain's secretaries to apologise that Brain had been too busy but that a drink may be possible in the future. Chambers was bemused and the visit never occurred. 'I am unclear about why he was so distanced from the congregation or whether that was by his design or by the NOS bureaucracy that surrounded him,' he says.

Paul Thomson sheds light on this area: 'Before we moved to Sheffield the concept of shielding Chris from the congregation was explained to me. Steve Williams, Jon Ingham and other leaders were supposed to protect him from direct criticism and adulation; they were supposed to be a buffer zone, to take the flak to allow Chris to continue his work unimpeded.' Williams says, 'We were there to protect Chris from congregation members, but on occasions he'd get this sort of communication from "outside" which would get him off guard. In the right mood, it brought out the very best in Chris, he was genuinely moved by the interest and concern of others, and keen to meet them.'

Others also report positive experiences with Brain. Kim Campbell, who was also on the periphery of NOS, had limited contacts with Brain which were helpful and constructive. Once, after a service, she asked him for advice on a personal decision concerning sexuality and he reacted with complete openness and simply asked if she had faith in her own decision. 'His response could not have been more empowering,' Campbell recalls. On another occasion after he preached about equality with leaders, Campbell went up to him and asked him directly why he sometimes appeared to stare with hostility at her during services. 'He seemed abashed, vulnerable and appeared to be searching himself; he was taken aback by the very idea of me thinking that he was staring at me in a hostile way,' she says. There was nothing to suggest that he was proud, manipulative or arrogant, Campbell explains; he respected her and considered her question seriously.

John Chambers believes that the manipulations and abuses levelled at Brain in his relationships need balancing against the congregational benefits of his acute insights into interpersonal communications. 'Because Chris was brilliant at cutting through bullshit, and deceptive, self-serving etiquette's; people didn't play games in NOS. There was a clear sense of taking responsibility, and being honest, rather than polite', he says. He remembers Brain stopping someone from self indulgently using an inappropriate meeting to air a personal grievance. 'The flip side of his manipulation was his insight and teaching on real, no nonsense, honesty, and that is something that I found refreshing at NOS', Chambers says. 'At NOS we didn't talk theology, or "Vision", we did it and this is largely through a commitment to honesty in communications and relationships, which I am sure came from Chris'.

Having created this phenomenal church, Brain and his leaders went on to create the structures to support it. Once again Brain was the main mover, using his gifted and creative team to set up the sort of 'management systems' that would reinforce the members' dependence on and commitment to the church. The sort of systems that shielded Brain from the congregation, whilst increasing his mystique and power. With the systems in place in the inner core of leaders (many of whom had given up their careers to get involved) Brain could use them to further his aims. The leaders were so wrapped up in the vision and their leader, so frightened of being attacked or excluded, that they rarely resisted Brain's plans. To do so meant rejection and expulsion, and that much they had no questions about.

4

All Roads Lead to Chris

As early as 1987, Robert Warren had become convinced that the NOS experiment was working. It was more than working, it was a startling success in terms of the rapidly expanding membership and the creative and efficient outworking of its ideas. Robert Warren agreed to continue it indefinitely, and to designate it as a separate congregation within St Thomas's. Warren was in fact a Team Rector and there were already three separate congregations meeting at different times of the day. The establishment of NOS as a separate church congregation led by Brain, working under Robert Warren, fitted directly into St Thomas structures. The NOS congregation, like those already in existence, had its own leader, a pastoral leader (Steve Williams), and a ministry leader (Sarah Collins).

There were several NOS members on St Thomas's Parochial Church Council, the parish church's chief democratic body, which functions (among other things) to protect congregations from wayward or extreme vicars or leaders. However, although NOS members were elected, most of the candidates were hand picked by Brain and were his supporters. Most churches would have other democratic structures within the church itself, but because Warren had given Brain the freedom to experiment he asked no questions of the leadership structure. Warren recalls: 'The leadership was very much focused around Chris, but nobody was complaining and it was an experiment so we gave them the benefit of the doubt.'

In fact, for all its talk about equality and community NOS was an extremely hierarchical organisation, with a complete absence of democratic structures, with Brain at the apex. There was an elaborate and formal structure to the organisation with two distinct strands. The primary strand was the community itself (now known as NOS Community) which incorporated ministry and support of its members, discipleship groups and other church structures, as well as minor social action initiatives within the locality. The secondary strand centred on the arts and included the band, the film team, the worship design team for the service, and the research work that fuelled the NOS vision.

In 1990, this separation was formalised and a charitable trust (focusing on the arts) was set up to facilitate the Nine O'Clock Service vision and to spread its experimental worship to their churches. It was called the Nine O'Clock Trust and was made up of five departments (Arts, Music, Touring, Administration and Fundraising) with up to forty staff members in each department with job descriptions varying from tape operator to slides team manager. Jon Ingham was the general manager, but as the Nine O'Clock Trust Teams List shows, Chris Brain (printed in upper case, and bold) was the founder. In effect, he had created another byzantine, hierarchical organisation that was completely dominated by him and which (as a charitable trust) was financially independent and not accountable to St Thomas's.

NOS was the church and the community, but the Nine O'Clock Trust had a higher status; it was the artists' forum. It was the radical mission department that assimilated information as well as made inroads into the culture via the multi-media services, and spread the vision to other interested churches.

The structure of NOS itself was, on the outside, along conventional lines, particularly for a large, lively and growing church based in the hierarchical charismatic tradition. It had discipleship group leaders who led small bible study and discussion groups, and leaders responsible for recruitment, ministry, and pastoral work, with Brain as the overall leader, albeit working under Warren, the Team Rector. However, to describe how this structure worked in practice it is best to outline the experiences of members as their involvement increased and they moved from tier to tier.

On first attending the church, newcomers would be met by one of 40 or 50 'sweepers' whose job was to find visitors, welcome them and invite them to fill in a visitor's card if they were interested in finding out more about the church. In fact the sweeper team was asked to target particular groups of people who they were supposed to recruit. Generally they were told to make contact with 'clubby' people. At one stage they were desperate to have more black people in the congregation, while at other times they targeted the poor. The rationale behind such selection procedures was that NOS was supposed to be an urban church for those who didn't fit into normal ecclesiastical structures. At times they saw themselves as overrun by students or charismatics wanting a day out.

After filling in a visitor's form, prospective members were visited by two 'welcome pastors'. Ostensibly their function was to inform the person about the church; in fact their job was to assess whether or not the person was 'right' for NOS. Although this was supposed to be 'discerned spiritually', sometimes they based the decisions on surface impressions and discussed them in the pub. The welcome pastors discussed the people that they had visited and the appropriate strategies for encouraging them to join or for putting them off.

Paul (not his real name) was a welcome pastor and he saw his job chiefly as vetting prospective members. The unwritten criterion for selecting prospective members was whether they were from club culture and whether they were 'cool'. After this style assessment (although other factors to do with commitment and sexual relationships played a part) about 70% of applicants dropped out. About half of those that didn't were turned away. If the welcome pastors deemed an individual fit the bill, then they explained the commitment involved in joining NOS fairly superficially. If they were from church culture and were considered a square peg in a cool hole then the welcome pastors stressed the commitments of joining NOS. Even to the feverishly eager, the NOS commitment was no laughing matter.

Prospective members were told about the importance of community and living a simple lifestyle. If they were unmarried the pleasures of celibacy were held out before them. They were told that they should only join NOS, if they were able to make a three year commitment (and possibly a lifetime one), and were willing to give financially and take on some form of ministry to serve the NOS vision. Welcome pastors were instructed to tell all new members who Brain was and to stress the accountability involved in joining, as in many charismatic churches accountability meant consulting over and obeying important decisions. For many this put them off, while for many others the welcome pastors simply refused membership. 'It was abusive, it was manipulative and patronising', Paul now says, adding: 'I cringe at our arrogance'. He remembers his own visit from the welcome pastor as akin to a job interview. He had to fill in a detailed form outlining his skills, his work and church experience that the recruitment department later used when asking him to fulfil various responsibilities. The decision to join this church was something to be taken seriously.

In some senses this unequivocal presentation of the demands that NOS would make, was honest and reflected the gravity and importance of joining the NOS community. It was a little like Jesus Christ's parable in which he stressed the difficulties and responsibilities of entering the Kingdom of God and urged serious consideration on people before taking the decision. John Chambers came through the Welcome procedure unscathed, but describes his flat-mate as shaking for hours after the first 'Welcome Interview'. Chambers says, 'He was severely shaken by the experience but that's not necessarily bad; I like the idea of a church which makes demands, which challenges people rather than pleading with them to join. Another consequence of such a rigorous vetting policy was that those who got through were likely to be zealots, or, at least, deeply committed to the cause.

However, those individuals that the sweepers located as having significant money or influence by-passed the welcome pastors, and were immediately introduced to the leadership team (but not Brain) and taken for meals or befriended and introduced to the vision. Paul says of the two tier entry system: 'I now realise that it reflected NOS's attitude completely. At the time I believed that it was a more efficient way of recruiting people and bringing people in to NOS, but really it showed that money and status were what NOS rated, others got treated quite differently.'

Once members had succeeded in joining they were assigned to a Discipleship Group of about twelve members, with a leader who they were accountable to pastorally. The discipleship group leader was responsible for keeping members of their groups on the 'straight and narrow'. They were the first line managers for the soul and were the people that should be approached if a member of the group was having problems, or if they had a major decision to make such as changing jobs or starting a relationship. They were, in effect, unqualified counsellors (though some were trained at their work), having to deal with the problems of their group members or creating problems based on the issues that NOS raised.

In the early years, NOS opposed bringing in outside agencies. They were still living out the dualism which believed that the world (and church) outside was contaminated. What members of the group didn't always realise was that serious information concerning personal problems could be passed on up the hierarchy to the pastoral leaders and beyond and was sometimes used against them. Pete (not his real name) who was a pastoral leader over several discipleship groups says: 'I was told by the leaders that all sexual issues had to be passed on to Chris. When I asked why I was told that it was because sexual sin is so dangerous to people physically, mentally and spiritually, and that he had to know because of the 'covering' in the Spirit that he gave to NOS.'

The discipleship group leader was also given teaching materials by the pastoral leader of the church, who in turn had guidance from Brain about exactly what the discipleship groups should be studying. However, the content of the study materials wasn't necessarily of primary importance. The skills of the discipleship leader in group dynamics were equally important. In effect, it was the discipleship group leader's job to manoeuvre situations within the group to bring up those issues which he or she felt that the individual members should be facing.

Carol was the youngest member of her group when she was made a group leader at 20. Steve Williams, head of the pastoral department trained her at group leaders' meetings. This training included a ten page booklet by Brain on coping with 'problem situations' as a discipleship group leader. Several of the methods he advocated are manipulative; all are based on the unwavering premise that the leader *knows* what the problematic member's difficulty is, and where they need to get to. According to Brain, when someone in the discipleship group is sharing in a way that is not 'productive' the leader should 'not reinforce the sharing! . . . avoid eye contact, close up body language, do not support where he or she is at.'

Twenty-year-old Carol was also trained in how to manage married couples in her group. 'I was trained in playing married couples off against each other. Whoever was dominant I would ignore, and the quieter one I had to affirm and encourage. The idea was to wind the dominant partner up, to bring issues to a head in their relationship', she says. Once issues were brought to a head, the all-knowing discipleship leader would confront the person with the issue and challenge them to change their behaviour. 'We were told that this was loving our group members because we were helping to make them whole', Carol explains. She adds: 'We were taught that loving aggressively was good, that we needed to be 100% totally committed or "full on" and that Christianity wasn't about being nice, but was about the "passionate fruits", the hard edged aspects of the Holy Spirit.'

It is unfair to say that the discipleship groups became encounter groups whose sole purpose was to force people to face their problems. They were also used for bible study, prayer and for socialising. People shared and were supported in this 'family' like environment but they were also challenged. Some leaders were also much gentler, more sensitive and discreet than others but the radical nature of the vision meant that this form of intrusive 'therapy' occurred regularly. Intrusive therapy was considered necessary, and not surprisingly, some people grew increasingly introspective, insecure and neurotic.

Paul considers his experience in a discipleship group as a catalogue of manipulation and damage. Having waited two months after his 'job interview' welcome session he was invited to join the discipleship group led by his elder brother Sean. Paul believes that this was a deliberate attempt to start him off in a debilitating, unhealthy dynamic, being pastored by his elder brother. It was a situation that he believes Brain (by placing him in that group) orchestrated specifically to make him face issues and to allow Brain to keep a close eye on Paul. When Paul complained about being under his elder brother's authority Brain told him that his relationship with his brother was being set up as an example to the church. 'I didn't see it as abusive then', Paul says, 'I saw it as challenging me on a deep level so that I could work more fully for the vision, but really it was an attempt to control me.' This challenging involved receiving frequent put downs and humiliations from his brother Sean, who was one of Brain's inner circle.

Sean, who was a member of the band, told his brother that he must give up his musical aspirations (Paul had played in bands for years), and that he must face his 'sexual fantasies' over female members of the band. Paul was unaware of having problems in these areas and found it particularly galling to be receiving these instructions from his brother, who he had never had an easy relationship with. He was also put in an impossible situation, having been instructed not to repress his supposed sexual fantasies but to bring them out and sort them out. Denying the existence of the fantasies would have been interpreted as repressing them whilst accepting and confessing them would have been untrue and would also have placed himself in a dependent and vulnerable situation.

Even more benign discipleship group leaders were in no doubt where their loyalty lay if a conflict of interest occurred between a member of their discipleship group and the leadership. One Sunday evening in 1989 Pete was confronted by Brain at the end of a service: 'Out of the blue, after the service finished, Chris turned and looked straight at me and stuck his finger in my face and said, "Why the hell do you think that you're better than anybody here?"' When Pete explained that he didn't think that: 'Brain then shouted, "Who the hell do you think you are? How dare you talk to me like that?" '

Sue (not her real name), his discipleship group leader at the time, was standing beside Pete and took him aside. Pete asked her why she didn't defend him. She explained that Pete was her friend but Brain was her leader. The next day, Pete says, Sue told him that he was too competitive and that Brain wasn't pleased with his behaviour. She took Brain's side and told Pete to face his competitive nature. During the following years Pete was constantly challenged over his competitive nature, to the extent that he became paranoid about it.

The next step up the pastoral ladder was to become a pastoral leader in charge of several discipleship group leaders, all working under Steve Williams, the head of the pastoral department. However, according to Pete, relationships could also be problematic between pastoral leaders, the pastoral head and others in authority. Pete is bisexual and believes that because of this he was chosen to lead men in their sexuality. He was surprised that many in the pastoral department seemed obsessed with sexuality and sexual fantasies. Pete says: 'Their interest was bizarre but I think that they wanted a bisexual leader to be radical or trendy.'

On returning from holiday Pete was upset by the memory of a sexual assault that he had narrowly escaped. He talked to people in the pastoral department about it and was told that it was his sinfulness that had led to this incident. It was something in his spirit, his mind and his body language that led to the disturbing events. Pete blamed himself and became depressed and reclusive, fearing that he might be spreading his sinfulness if he socialised.

Pete made the mistake of becoming involved with another member of the congregation without his pastoral leader's permission. Some time later he got her pregnant. Pete asked to see his pastoral leader seeking support and advice. He recalls: 'Williams shouted at me, telling me that I was the most unaccountable person he'd ever met and that I did not realise the damage I had done.' Williams says: 'From my point of view this is a very partial version of the situation, I'm not known for shouting.' From this point on Pete believes that he was deliberately isolated and that his friends were told not to see him. He went through years of self loathing and attempted suicide three times. Pete says: 'My point is that the leadership did not give a damn about me. Their pick-and-mix theology, counselling and personal confusion was projected on to the congregation and did severe damage to me.'

Others in NOS testify to being encouraged in this sort of paranoia. Car accidents or near misses were often interpreted as being a sign of sin or unresolved issues. One member relates an occasion when Brain told her that her sin caused a friend to have a serious bike accident. She lived in fear of having permanently damaged her friend. According to Pete, members of the pastoral department told him not to take someone to hospital who was on the verge of suicide; it had to be sorted out in house. He says: 'This person was in a seriously bad way. She claimed to have taken some tablets and I had a row with members of the pastoral team about it. In the end I took her. They thought that they were best qualified to deal with such cases because they knew the people, although they had no professional training.'

One other NOS structure that had a controlling influence on people was the recruitment department. Although this was a part of the NOS church it also served the Nine O'Clock Trust. When team leaders (from NOS or the Trust) needed some additional staff they would explain their needs to the recruitment department who would locate suitable people, consult with their discipleship group leader about their current attitude and outlook, and then approach them to talk about the possibility of taking on the responsibility.

The recruitment structure was designed to channel members in the direction where they could be of most use to NOS and the

Trust. In effect it made decisions on behalf of the members. Many churches work on the basis that people are drawn to particular ministries (as their 'calling') and consequently approach the leadership about getting involved. NOS's model was almost diametrically opposite. Expressing an interest in a ministry was likely to be interpreted as egoistic power seeking, thereby precluding one from working in the desired area until various issues had been faced. Chambers presents this approach positively: 'I really liked the way NOS found out what you were good at and then asked you to do something totally different for a year. To get a singer cleaning, or a police officer in a sound studio helps to break the connection between a person's identity or value and their job or role'. Although people's 'calling' was often discussed, the decisions and direction that they took would be decided from on high.

There was another aspect of NOS and the Nine O'Clock Trust that made it incredibly confusing for those that weren't within the inner core of the NOS leadership team. This was a culture of almost obsessive secrecy. New projects would be set up and the personnel to carry out the project recruited and told (for a number of reasons) not to tell others what they were working on. These people were, for a while, a privileged elite, whilst those outside were left guessing and were made to feel that they weren't trusted.

It was not uncommon for staff members not to know who was working in what role. This was exacerbated by regular reshuffles of personnel. Almost as soon as new lists of personnel were typed up, they were out of date. According to Pauline (not her real name), a member who worked in NOS's administration department, it was almost impossible to keep track of who was doing what and for how long. She says: 'There was so much that we simply weren't allowed to know, either about the Trust or the finances or about new ventures. It was bewildering.' It is quite possible that the pace of change was a manipulative tool used by Brain to keep people either bewildered or on their toes.

Fiona, who worked in the trust finance team, adds: 'Chris appeared to decide who was to be released to work in various areas on a whim.' When Fiona was leading the Trust finance department she broke the code of secrecy to her cost. She was supposed to be overseeing a team who were raising funds for the Trust, from outside donors and members of the congregation. She was continually frustrated because the trust leaders wouldn't tell her what they were actually raising funds for. She felt that a fundraising team couldn't elicit money unless they could give donors some idea of what the funds were to be used for. Eventually she got access to some of the details and at the team's next meeting she passed on the details to them. When the leaders found out what had happened they gave her a severe dressing down. Brain then approached Elizabeth, another Trust worker, to do the job and days later Fiona discovered that she was no longer in the post. However, others had been told that Fiona was no longer in the post because of 'pastoral problems'.

The finances of NOS and the Trust (although Trust accounts were audited and published) appear to have been shrouded in secrecy. At some stages, Fiona recalls, Trust members weren't allowed to process accounts in a NOS room. She says: 'I was constantly attacked because I didn't accept the fact that we had to be so secretive about finance. There was a lot of effort put into obscuring the reality of the Trust finance by careful presentation.' Fiona believes that the secrecy around finance was to disguise exactly how much money was being put at the disposal of Brain. According to Fiona, by 1992 approximately 25% of the congregation's donations to the Trust (not including large capital gifts) went into Brain's expenses budget for his work promoting the NOS vision. It funded 'team building' trips to Alton Towers from Brain's research and training budget, and his car, mobile phone and meals at a designated restaurant. This was all legal (the Trust finances were given a clean bill of health by lawyers following the revelations in August 1995) but Fiona believes that Brain's forceful personality may have led to the Trust justifying things that with hindsight, they may not have agreed to.

However, donations given to Brain by congregation members funded his luxurious lifestyle. He wanted more money from the Trust to fund what he called his 'entrepreneurial style of ministry' but was told to seek it elsewhere because the Trust could not justify requests for funds that weren't within their remit. Over the years Brain had shown himself to be skilful at persuading those around him to make regular gifts for his personal use. These gifts varied between hundreds of pounds and tens of thousands.

Brain ate out at restaurants several days each week, invariably wore designer clothes and visited France, Spain, New York and California. His Victorian townhouse was a statement of upmarket interior design sense with no expense spared. A NOS member who worked decorating it was surprised by the plushness of the decor and the amount of trouble that was put into the smallest detail. 'In 1990, £30 and countless hours were spent finding the right pedal bin for the kitchen. It was colour co-ordinated, easily the plushest house I'd ever worked on, ' he says.

Secrecy appears to have reached almost paranoid proportions when staff members were sent to outside organisations to carry out 'research'. Pauline was set a research project by NOS leaders. Her task was to find out about a high profile charity's publicity machine, what strategies did they use which made their communications with the media so successful? Pauline interviewed members of their public relations team over a number of days. However, she was told (as researchers always were) to try and avoid revealing what organisation she was working for. She said that she was a student working for a multi-media arts foundation, and carried out her researches and reported back. People in the leadership who asked for such research projects often seemed reluctant to let outsiders know information about NOS or the Trust. Pauline says that this also affected social situations: 'I felt that we were supposed to be extremely careful about how we represented NOS, as though the leaders had to control the image.'

The secrecy was also clearly at work in dealing with outsiders inquiring about NOS. Journalists were unwittingly manipulated into writing the sort of articles that the leadership team had decided that they wanted at particular times. A list of journalists was kept and decisions were taken about exactly what line they would feed to them. Meticulous points were typed out and given to the journalists, outlining the agenda that NOS wanted them to pursue. The image of NOS was something that, not unreasonably, they wanted control over. But although leadership members were friendly with media contacts, journalists and photographers were frequently taken aback at the amount of control they wanted. Journalists were also made to feel privileged to be given access to Brain. He was completely unknown but trying to interview him was a bit like trying to interview Elvis back from the grave.

In 1991, when I was researching a feature on NOS for *The Times*, I was introduced to the press officer and head of communications, then to Brain's PA, before being taken into a darkened room with a weird film loop with obscure symbols projected on a wall. Behind a black table, Brain sat with black minders on either side. I was told that I was one of hundreds of media enquiries and the others had been rejected. Possibly the intention was to unnerve or impress and the whole situation seemed stage managed and controlled. A great deal of thought had been put into both the information that I received and the impression that I was given. In the event Brain was personable, quick thinking and interesting, even if he and his entourage displayed an unnerving tendency to take themselves far too seriously. Like everyone else I explained away my doubts (about their utter seriousness) with the magnitude of the 'vision'.

Church leaders had no more success in getting to the heart of NOS. Robert Warren, who first gave NOS the go-ahead, explains that although he had immense respect for Brain in the early days it was hard to be included in what was going on. 'Through an interplay of flattery and remarks that left one feeling inadequate and uncomfortable, he kept us marginalised; we were never allowed into the inner workings of the congregation', he says. He remembers there was particular secrecy surrounding the finances and suspects that the trust may have been formed partly to avoid inquiries into how money was being used.

Stephen Lowe, Archdeacon of Sheffield, who regularly attended NOS in the later years (from 1993) and found it deeply inspiring, had little success in penetrating the veil of secrecy. Lowe was always met by intermediaries rather than Brain and he says that he was usually met by Elizabeth who was his main point of contact between the Church of England and NOS and the Trust. He says: 'She was quite difficult to deal with because one day she'd be warm and open and the next she'd be inexplicably cold and I'd feel that I'd made some gaffe but she was always fiercely protective of Chris and NOS.' On his rare meetings with Brain, Lowe feels that Brain's mind games always deflected any inquiries. 'I always left a meeting with Chris feeling drained, as if he had been feeding off me, constantly asking me theological and pastoral questions', he says, adding: 'After a meeting with Chris I invariably left feeling a failure. I had a sense of how out of touch I was with club culture and, very subtly, I was made to feel it.'

Professor John Rogerson, Head of Sheffield University's Biblical Studies Department, was also taken in by Brain. He regularly taught at the services and was for a time a member of a discipleship group but was completely shocked when the stories of abuse surfaced in August 1995. He had joined NOS in 1992 because he was attracted by what appeared to be a grassroots community working out an authentic way of Christian living in a postmodern context. He never saw much of Brain but says: 'My impression was of a shadowy figure in the background, an uneducated young man with working class roots who was catalysing some of my most able students to create this innovative church that was totally unlike anything I'd ever seen before.' His view of the service in the later years was that it was stylistically brilliant and that it was drawing together a number of theological strands into an apparently vibrant whole, but that many of the strands were incompatible.

However, although outside clergy were flattered, involved and beguiled, Brain appears to have felt threatened by their involvement. On the one hand he publicised their endorsement and enthusiasm for NOS, presumably as a way of reaffirming the service's credibility and importance. On the other hand he made sure that those in leadership were deeply suspicious of these outside authorities. He derided them behind their backs and suggested that they had hidden agendas. This perception trickled down to ordinary members. Alan Gibson recalls: 'Robert Warren and St Thomas's were set up as enemies so that members wouldn't complain to Warren. Bishop Lunn and the archdeacon were incredibly supportive of the vision but they were also set up as potential enemies; the unspoken message being that people shouldn't take their concerns or complaints to them because if they did then the outsiders would step in and take too much control in the running of NOS.'

Sarah Collins was told that she was on a power trip when Brain discovered that she had independently contacted Graham Cray, then the vicar of St Michael-le-Belfrey and member of NOS's advisory group. She was told not to do so again. Stephen Lowe says that Brain told other members of the leadership team that he was trying to get hold of NOS money for the diocese. Leaders were confused when Lowe started giving his own money to the service, rather than to the diocese.

Not surprisingly, with this sort of secrecy surrounding the leadership and the decision making processes, members of the congregation became frustrated. This was particularly true of people like Alan Gibson, Mark Estdale and Mel Lloyd who wanted NOS to get involved in social action projects in inner city Sheffield. The leadership clearly picked up on the disquiet of the membership because at some point in 1990 Alan Gibson was phoned by one of Brain's secretaries and asked to produce a report on what the congregation's questions were. He reported to Brain and his leaders with a list of questions and it was decided to hold a congregational meeting at Sheffield City Hall in which Gibson would ask the leaders the questions.

The main questions concerned what the leadership roles were and who were the leaders, what the Nine O'Clock Trust was and what it did, and how money was used and who made the decisions concerning its use. According to Gibson: 'A central question was why there was so much secrecy in NOS.' The answer given was that there wasn't and that the leaders would seek to improve their communications.

Although some questions were answered adequately (lists of leaders and their responsibilities, for instance) others were fudged and, despite having two congregational meetings for questions, they never got on to answering the financial questions. Gibson stresses that this needn't have necessarily been a cover up, so much as the arrogance of Brain and his leaders, who may have felt that they had answered enough questions. Whatever the answer to this, there was no improvement in communications, no improved transparency and the secrecy continued.

In September 1990 Chris stood down from the running of NOS to take ordination training on the Northern Ordination Course based in Leeds. Although he stayed at his Parkers Road house in Sheffield, he distanced himself from the running of the church. He left the church in the trusted hands of his two right hand men: Steve Williams was left in charge of NOS and Jon Ingham was left in charge of the Trust. Ingham recalls: 'We were instructed to duplicate what was going on, to train leaders and to build up resources.' He adds: 'We had no power to change things, if decisions needed taking, we had to consult Chris.'

Meanwhile, Brain was the apple of everyone's eye, whilst he studied in luxurious isolation with one hand firmly on the tiller. Despite his lower profile during his studies, clearly the leaders and members of the congregation still served his needs. All roads still led to Chris.

5

The Postmodern Nuns

In September 1990, when Brain left to train to become a priest, he did so with the full support of Robert Warren, Graham Cray and others. He had been through the normal Anglican selection procedures for ordinands, including detailed references and a lengthy interview process with Trevor Page, the Director of Ordinands for the Diocese of Sheffield. On a selection conference with other potential ordinands, Brain was interviewed about his sense of calling, pastoral approach, prayer life and worship. He was involved in group exercises, had to lead a discussion and was observed worshipping. Brain was an enthusiastic candidate with excellent credentials as the leader of a five hundred strong church. According to Lowe, when Brain was asked questions concerning sexual behaviour and ethics, his response was: 'It doesn't seem to matter where you stand on sexual matters in the Church of England provided that you are left wing politically. In NOS we are very different. We do not mind what way you vote but we expect the highest standards of sexual behaviour.' Once again, Brain seems to have known what to say to reassure and impress. There was nothing in Brain's behaviour which suggested that he wasn't a suitable candidate for ordination.

Brain started to attend the three year course and Michael Williams, the course principal, was positive about the quality of his work and participation. What Williams didn't know was that Brain's essays were, in fact, written by theology graduates within NOS who acted as his academic mentors during the course. It is difficult to know whether Brain got NOS members to write his essays because he was not confident of his own intellectual or academic powers, or whether he was too busy, or lazy, to write them himself. One of his mentors believes that Brain wasn't necessarily academically brilliant, but was a genius at synthesising other people's thinking and creativity. She also points out that he told her that he had Michael Williams' permission for others to work on his essays, which was not the case. So what *did* Brain do during his part time three year course? 'He spent a lot of time reading books as well as manipulating and controlling those around him', she says. He also spent considerable time setting up what was to be known as the Homebase Team.

Fellow students on the Northern Ordination Course recall that at the residential summer school he appeared unusually homesick for someone in their thirties. A course member who trained alongside him felt that he seemed uneasy socially. 'He didn't really integrate with the group, I felt that he wasn't sure of himself. He seemed vulnerable and withdrawn', she recalls. During coffee breaks between lectures Brain would sit alone reading a book rather than chatting with the other ordinands. Despite this apparent shyness, during debates Brain would name-drop various senior theologians that he had been talking to. In intellectual debate Brain came to life, but as a human being he was impossible to penetrate.

It was during this time that Winnie Brain got pregnant. Despite the fact that Brain had been relieved from the responsibilities of running NOS and that his ordination course was designed for people with full time jobs, he decided that Winnie and he needed domestic and practical help around the house so that he could adequately concentrate on his studies. One member started to help with cooking, shopping, cleaning and trying to befriend Winnie, who she felt was often ignored by the people who were desperate to befriend her husband. She often stayed over at their house and saw it as straight forward Christian service. Others were occasionally doing their gardening.

However, Brain felt the need for more help and he started assembling a team of women and one man, who could help with duties around the house. Some of the women he recruited were women who he had been sexually involved with. One congregation member was groomed for Homebase by Brain but was dropped when she rejected Brain's physical advances because he said that he couldn't trust her close to him as her boundaries were too pronounced. Others were more compliant and found themselves on the Homebase Team, confused about Brain but trusting that somehow he must be pure and interpreting their misgivings about his behaviour as their own problem.

This sort of sexual manipulation appears to have been quite normal for Brain. With virtually all the women he had close contact with he would start to blur the boundaries between friendship and romantic or sexual contact. This sometimes started with asking people to discuss their sexual fantasies or problems, or making ambiguous and risqué remarks to them, or by asking them to massage him or to stroke his hair. It was not uncommon for Brain to place his head in women's laps and ask for a massage. Possibly it was a risk free way of gauging how open they were to his sexual advances. Occasionally women completely rejected him and he knew not to try it again.

Mel Lloyd was a discipleship group leader when Brain placed his head in her lap and requested a massage. She felt uncomfortable and said so. According to Lloyd, Brain then said: 'Is that a "f---k off Chris" then?' She agreed and he never put her in a sexually compromising situation again. Others were more compliant, but feeling awkward, managed to communicate their sexual boundaries. Brain had already manoeuvred Pauline into sharing her sexual history with him. 'From my first meeting with Chris he appeared to hold strong views about how I should be conducting my relationships with men and expressing my sexuality, and his prescriptive advice came to form the basis of my relationship with him over the next few years', she says. He asked her to trust him, which she did, and she made some major decisions about her life in the light of his directive 'pastoring'.

On one occasion when she walked into a room where he was sitting he held his arm out for Pauline to come and embrace him. When she did he put his head against her stomach and started rubbing her legs and thighs. Pauline felt some uneasiness about being in a situation in which such physical intimacy hadn't been negotiated, but started massaging his shoulders. On another occasion he whacked her backside with a ruler and Pauline turned round and glared at him. Brain, slightly taken aback, reminded her of the trust she had said that she had in him and effectively excused himself of any offence that he had caused, leaving Pauline feeling guilty about her reaction. Later, in a conversation with Pauline, he told her that he wasn't sure that he liked her, partly due to her physical boundaries, which he saw as 'walls' that she erected around herself.

Marion (not her real name) joined NOS in 1986 and married Greg two years later. Greg was involved with leadership and the couple holidayed with the Brains on the south coast, early in their involvement with NOS. Later Brain distanced himself from her and every so often he would ask her why they weren't such good friends anymore, suggesting that it was a deliberate move on her part. Whenever Marion tried to improve relations, Brain would make her feel awkward. 'My friendship with Chris became an underlying problem in my life which I kept unsuccessfully trying to sort out. Whenever I phoned, his secretary passed me on to his personal assistant, who said that he was busy; he kept me at arms length but feeling that it was my problem', she says. After a time Brain started hugging Marion, then cuddling, then kissing her, explaining all along that it was an expression of friendship. 'That was the currency by which people knew whether they were his friends or not', Marion explains. She remembers: 'For such an unemotional person he was always quite cuddly. Then he'd kiss me and I'd freeze to stop it going any further.'

On one occasion Brain invited Greg and Marion round for tea. Winnie was cooking downstairs and Brain shouted down for Marion to come up to his bedroom. He was lying on his bed with only a dressing gown on and he asked for a cuddle. 'He acted as if this was completely normal for those around him but I felt that it was different, I was uncomfortable so I was lukewarm with him', Marion explains. Partly because of Marion's suspicions of Brain and her increasingly questioning attitude towards the NOS vision, she became largely sidelined. Greg, however, was an arty, enthusiastic member of the leadership team and it wasn't long before Brain started trying to play them off against each other, suggesting to Greg that Marion was resisting God's will.

Perhaps in desperation, after a couple of years without contact, Brain phoned Marion one evening and asked her to come around. He asked her to relax and lie down and turned the meeting into an impromptu therapy session, talking about Marion's coldness and how out of touch she was with her feelings and sexuality. He started to caress and cuddle her and Marion became increasingly unresponsive. Brain then said: 'Why is it that you repress your sexuality?' Marion sat up and said without irony: 'Basically whenever I act sexy I get abused.' Although she wasn't referring to Brain, Marion now believes that he thought she was. He immediately changed tack and started talking about their friendship.

Steve Williams, who was head of the pastoral department, believes Brain had a psychological need to sexually dominate women and for women to find him sexually attractive. He says: 'The basis of his confidence in his ability to control groups of people appeared to revolve around his personal sexual charisma and he needed to know that everyone found him attractive and would make sure that they did.' He refers to Brain's methods of doing this as his 'grooming process', and saw it happen on many occasions, although he only realised the true nature of what was going on after he left NOS in 1993. Obviously, it was different for each individual, but Williams describes the hallmarks of the process as follows.

Initially Brain would praise them, telling them that there was no one else like them, and that they were his Mary Magdalene. If they were married (or had a boyfriend) he would tell them that their spouse or boyfriend was holding them back spiritually and that he would help them to be released from their exploitation and suggest himself as a healthier male role model. He would offer them affection without sex, but tell them that they were free to do certain things although they shouldn't tell their partners for fear of misunderstandings. Brain would then frequently approach the husband and tell them of the spiritual and psychological work that he was engaged on with their wives or girlfriends, offering to do for their partners what he had done for others. He would ask for their blessing, and if they refused he would verbally attack them as sexist, reactionary, possessive males.

The next stage was to spend money on the women, to buy them clothes and to take them for meals and to introduce them to other women within his circle, including women from what was to become the Homebase Team. He would then build up late night counselling sessions, which led on to massage and greater sexual involvement. As time went on the women often started to have doubts about what was happening, to which Brain would respond forcefully, reassuring them that he was helping them. If they tried to avoid him he would isolate them socially by removing their other responsibilities within NOS from them. Ultimately, he would treat them to the full force of his anger and swear them to secrecy. At this point, Williams explains, he was often brought in to 'sort out their issues' and to reintegrate them back to normality.

In summer 1990 about half a dozen young women who had agreed to help the Brains were called to a meeting in the Trust's

Mulehouse Road offices by Steve Williams. Most of these women were already close to Brain, deeply committed to the NOS vision and significantly under his influence. They were told that they were to be postmodern nuns who would act as support to allow the Brains to carry on their mission work. As nuns, like nearly all the women in leadership, they were to be celibate (unless married) and to perform an unassuming, home making role. The 'postmodern' prefix was presumably little more than a credible soundbite. The concept was never explained to the women involved, although it was demanded that they all dress 'of the culture' but were also to make themselves distinctive as a group. No one in the radical supposedly feminist orientated leadership asked why the members of the homemaking team were nearly all women (unusually attractive women too).

Tony was the one male on the team and he gave help with styling a postmodern nun's outfit. In the early days they wore black rave gear, lycra, leggings and/or miniskirts, black hair and strong make-up. The team were told that they had to be at the cutting edge of fashion trends, so their apparel changed over time. Steve Williams remembers them as what he calls 'clones of Winnie', who, he believes, were designed to fulfil Brain in areas that Winnie wasn't able to. He describes them as a composite personality created to reflect aspects of Winnie's personality that were absent.

They were to be called the Homebase Team. Those that had other responsibilities within NOS were relieved of their posts, withdrawn from discipleship groups and given their own pastor, who initially was Sarah Collins. It was never fully explained to them, but being on the Homebase Team meant withdrawing from outside social contacts; although they didn't live with the Brains they were discouraged from maintaining outside contacts and were frequently challenged by Brain about them. If they saw friends from the church there was an understanding that they weren't to discuss Homebase, it was considered prying into Brain's private life. One member who decorated at the Brains' house describes the bizarre situation in which he worked for weeks without a word being exchanged, presumably because they had been instructed not to talk to him. Like nuns, they were to become a secluded and secretive community.

However, this secretive community was to be at the heart of the abuse within NOS. Most members entered the Homebase Team as ordinary young women in the early 1990s and left, when the scandals surfaced in August 1995, as damaged people struggling to maintain their humanity and identity. There are different opinions about whether Brain surrounded himself with people who were besotted with him or wanted the status of being seen so close to him, or whether they were genuinely seeking to serve the Brains out of their Christian commitment.

Anita Hurding, who was close to the Brains and saw members of the Homebase Team regularly, says: 'Being on the Homebase Team was *the* status ministry, everyone wanted to be on it; it was the thing to aspire to and the people close to Chris got self esteem from it. If you were on the Homebase Team you'd made it.' Steve Williams confirms this: 'There was a queue of women waiting to get in to Homebase; if you were close to Chris Brain your status rocketed.' Some members of the congregation describe them as being aloof, arrogantly uncommunicative and self centred, once they had reached the pinnacle of being accepted on the Homebase Team.

Luke (not his real name), one of the NOS's leadership team, believes that they had genuinely selfless motives for joining and that they had their personalities severely damaged due to their proximity to Brain. He believes that their time as postmodern nuns was hell, and says: 'They were hammered, they were slaves, sometimes they got ten hour bollockings and were deliberately humiliated in front of others.' He also counters the idea that they were stuck up, vain or in love with Brain: 'They were rendered absolutely powerless . . . they were at the heart of a cult. They were sexually involved and manipulated but taught to believe that it would bring them wholeness. They had hell and lived in fear of Brain, by who they were manipulated into an obsessive dependence.'

Whatever motivated their involvement, their duties became clear in days after joining. They started going to the Brains' Parkers Road house before Ruth Brain was born, helping with cooking and cleaning and getting to know Winnie Brain. After Ruth's birth a rota was drawn up which delineated the team's responsibilities. It included cooking, cleaning, shopping, looking after Ruth, walking the dog, doing a 'sleepover' in case Ruth woke up. Putting Brain to bed was another of their tasks although (perhaps because several women who weren't on Homebase also did this job) there was no strict rota for this — it was based on Brain's whims. The idea behind putting Brain to bed was that he was so stressed from his work that each evening he needed a massage (often more than a massage but not full sex) to prepare him for sleep. In practice, this had been going on informally for years. Brain would phone people or pick them up in his car and ask them if they would put him to bed.

The Homebase Team soon got used to their long hours. As time passed they were increasingly spoken to and treated as servants. Visitors relate tales of coming round and seeing the Homebase Team ignored or unceremoniously ordered around like servants. Outsiders describe them as being so cowed and repressed as people that they were like little animals, beavering around selflessly then scuttling off whenever Brain told them to. However, their worst treatment was psychological, and sexual intimacy was the vehicle that Brain sometimes used. The sexual boundaries gradually eroded, at different rates with different people. It was normal to meet Brain's needs whilst putting him to bed and the very least that this meant was massaging him as he lay (often naked) in bed. What started as kissing and cuddling soon became heavy petting and by the time the NOS scandal broke, some members felt that he had complete control over their bodies.

Christine (not her real name), another member of the Homebase Team, has spoken of becoming psychologically and emotionally completely under Brain's control. She was initially taken into the vision via the usual route of the 'inspiring vision', leading to 'crossing cultures', followed by deeper involvement as she took on responsibilities. She attended the meeting which introduced the Homebase Team's role and understood it as being based on an ancient monastic order 'where the monks went out on mission and the nuns cared for them and looked after their needs when they got back.' No one seems to have seen a contradiction between sexist stereotypes being reinforced and Brain regularly challenging Homebase women about being bimbos and basing their identity on male expectations (known as objectifying).

Christine also had putting-to-bed duties and was offered sexual healing. She explains how she was led to understand it: 'He would teach me to discover my potential as a woman. I would come into sexual wholeness through allowing him to help me to it.' With time, the sexual encounters grew more extreme: 'It escalated from something I found acceptable . . . to something, in the end, that I now find unbelievable.' She adds: 'I also feel that in some way he owned my body; I was his to do what he wanted with.' Christine says she has been deeply damaged: 'It has cost me dearly, very dearly. I know that that's going to stay with me whatever I do.' She believes that Brain led her into a strange and damaging unreality. 'I now believe', she says, 'that I lived in a fantasy created by a severely deluded man for many years and he treated us like pawns for his own ends in what became a nightmare to me.'

Nadia (not her real name), another member of the Homebase Team, felt that she had to please Chris to please God. The sexual implications of this were clear. 'At first he was just being friendly, showing love as a friend and then it became a healing thing for me because I was so under confident in my sexuality and as a woman', she says. She was the youngest member of the Homebase Team and had had no prior sexual experience. She adds: 'He was the first person I'd ever been sexual with and I feel that, because that was abusive, I will find it hard to trust any man. I think it will take me a long time to believe that someone isn't just after sex and my body.' By the end of her experience on the Homebase Team, Nadia was in a severe psychological state. 'Through the whole spectrum of abuse I got depressed. I started not sleeping well and losing my appetite for weeks on end, getting suicidal', she says. She had lost her identity and her relationship with God. 'By the end of it I'd totally lost a sense of who I was, I was living in some void away from the real me. I certainly didn't know God any more', she recalls.

Brain frequently confronted members of the Homebase Team with issues that he felt they needed to face. Nadia's worst experience of this occurred when Brain suggested she start wearing make-up again because the natural look, he said, was passé. The Homebase Team were told that culturally they should look right together. Brain had told Nadia that she should be trying to look like a postmodern cyborg. They went upstairs to look through various *Face* magazines at women with similar shaped faces, to try and decide what would look right. Nadia was nervous because she had been verbally attacked many times about competing with Lori Camm (a female leader who appeared to be Brain's confidante and closest friend) and she was determined not to do so. She worried because she was aware of it, and Brain would interpret this awareness as a sign of competing. Brain turned to her and said: 'Are you all right, you seem nervous?'

Nadia explained that she was nervous because in the past (as Brain had forced her to admit many times) she had competed with Lori. Brain said that the nervousness proved that she must be competing but Nadia promised that she wasn't and they carried on looking through magazines until he decided that she needed some new lipstick. Nadia was told to join Lori downstairs and to go out with her to buy some lipstick. Minutes later he came down, fixed Nadia with a hostile stare and said: 'You're still nervous aren't you? You're still competing with Lori aren't you, you f---ing bitch! How can you still be doing that after all Lori's help to try and help you to become yourself? Lori could trash you in an instant and she holds back that power all the time, to allow you to be yourself.' He then told her that with all the best make-up artists and designers in the world she couldn't be as attractive as Lori was even when she wasn't trying.

As always happened Nadia gave in and apologised to Camm. Nadia was so obsessed with this supposed competition with Camm that each day she used to write out lists of things that Camm was good at that she could never do. She was told that the best way to deal with her competition was to affirm Camm, particularly in front of others. Nadia says: 'It got harder and harder to apologise to Lori because although I thought that they must be right, I felt angry.' Nadia was confronted about her persistent competitiveness for over five hours, with Brain continually asking: 'Why are you still doing it?' Brain and Camm wouldn't let go of the issue as Nadia begged them to forgive her and let her have another go. She confessed that she must be so opposed to the vision because every day she tried to overcome her competitiveness and every day she competed, and her abasement and apologies, she said, must sound like insults after she'd let them down so many times. Brain replied: 'F--- off, we don't want to hear your lists and apologies.'

Nadia stood there silent and contrite whilst Brain and Camm discussed her. Then Brain said: 'Look at her, she's power battling.' Nadia started crying and Brain said: 'Stop f---ing crying, we're the ones who should be crying, we're the ones that you've been utterly abusive to. How dare you cry, you're being f---ing manipulative.' Nadia recalls: 'I was in a complete state, I just stood there looking at the ground for half an hour.' Then Brain said that there was something that Nadia knew that she had to say to sort things out. Nadia had no idea what it was, she'd tried everything. Brain said if she wasn't going to do it she should walk off, go and be a bimbo, leave Ruth (the baby, who was Nadia's main Homebase responsibility), NOS, her friends, faith and everything that she believed. Then Brain and Camm left the room.

'I was standing there like a statue for 20 minutes before I had the courage to leave the house and to go across the road to my house', Nadia recalls. She saw no option except to leave NOS, but to do so was severely traumatic, because Brain had regularly told her that she had so much sin that she could die of cancer unless she dealt with it. In desperation, she went to her house nearby, phoned her parents and arranged to get a train home. When Brain and Camm realised that Nadia had left, Camm went to her house and was much gentler with her. Camm asked Nadia what she wanted and Nadia responded saying that she needed to loosen her relationship with Brain, she needed space to sort out her problems. She returned and Brain was there with tears in his eyes. He took a much softer line, reassured her and the flashpoint passed. Later Brain suggested to Nadia that her problems were to do with another issue and suggested that she phone her parents to explain and reassure them. Nadia stayed on the Homebase Team until the NOS scandal surfaced in 1995.

The psychological abuse was often extreme. Members of Homebase were continually confronted with things in their lives that Brain told them needed facing. Much of Brain's thinking was influenced by the theories of two American addiction therapists and cultural commentators, Ann Wilson-Schaef and Pia Mellody. Their theories were about how society encourages addictive behaviours, particularly for women. The barrage of glamorous images of women in magazines and TV led to women seeking their self esteem from male approval (looking good is feeling good), rather than from a process of self definition based on personal integrity. Increasingly Brain spoke psychobabble as well as fire and brimstone. He liked buzzwords like 'co-dependence', 'projection', 'externalising' and 'objectifying', which became common parlance on Homebase and around the NOS community. As usual, Brain drew on interesting and pertinent cultural thinking and skewed it to his own ends.

He would either find people's weaknesses and exploit them, or nurture a neurosis which allowed him to plant suggested weaknesses in the person concerned. Then gradually he would make them acknowledge these weaknesses, turning the ratchet further each time, until he would be screaming at them to sort themselves out or face expulsion from Homebase, or leadership, or his friendship. He tended to confront Homebase members with the same issues (perhaps depending on what he was reading) at the same time. He also went through phases concerning who he wanted on 'putting to bed' duties.

Although I have spoken to members of the Homebase Team, understandably they are reluctant for the details of what went on to be publicly known. It is, thus, hard to explain what held these women's loyalties and there are different explanations of it. Anita Hurding says: 'Why did they compromise themselves? The obvious answer is because of the status it gave them. They need to look at themselves as well as what Chris did to them; it's never that one sided.' Concerning their abuse, she says: 'No one gets into that sort of dynamic without getting something from it to make up for the pain.' Others suggest that Brain surrounded himself with 'lycra lovelies' who were desperate to be close to him and therefore not much manipulation was needed to get their compliance and obedience.

Linelle (not her real name), a theologian, who was on the Homebase Team and who has maintained some contact with Brain, stresses that issues to do with exploring the boundaries of sexuality were often discussed within the Homebase Team, and that the women were clear that an intimate relationship with Brain was not just for itself but in the context of a wider theological vision. 'We were participating in a work for Christ, to explore intimacy that included affection, expression of sexuality and sexual boundaries within friendship, that was good and whole and stood alongside marriage relationships', she says. Indeed, early on in her intimate relationship with Brain he told her to use the quality of her relationship with her husband as a barometer for how damaging or life enhancing, their experimentation was. 'As sexual expression evolved within our friendship', she says, 'Chris always accepted my caution; in fact he told me that I had to have a heightened sense of my integrity and moral awareness, and not to let go of this because I was getting pleasure, esteem and affection from our intimacy.' Linelle says that Brain was very clear that her integrity must be maintained.

Linelle and her husband believe that Brain has had a beneficial effect on their relationship and they question the reaction of the congregation to Brain, since the scandal surfaced. 'It's simply not as black and white as people are presenting it. Chris is not an angel but there's a lynch mob mentality which I am sceptical of', she says. The sudden shift in the congregation's feelings about Brain, Linelle says, is due to a deadly cocktail within his personality. 'His gifted, charismatic leadership and creative genius didn't mix well with the position of power that he was placed in', she says. Linelle believes Brain's problems with power were partly because people let him dominate. She points out that on occasions he cried out for help, seemingly wanting to offload his power and responsibility. But from within this internal struggle, she believes he found it impossible to relinquish his power. Ultimately, Linelle asserts that in the area of sexuality, Brain never treated her with anything but respect, but she has some legitimate complaints about how he treated her as a friend and a Homebase worker: 'He had evident weaknesses, and was sometimes high handed and abusive as a manager and friend, but his sensitivity to the planet and to justice was, in my view, sincere.'

Tony offers a different view, although he admits that his experience as the only male on the team was vastly different from the others. He believes that the abuse meted out to the Homebase Team was as extreme as the worst within NOS. As a male he was partly kept in the dark. He saw Brain kissing and cuddling women occasionally, which surprised him, but he is clear that he was only allowed to see the tip of the iceberg. He says: 'Most of the time people were hung up and strung out, the tension was extreme and it was a result of living in fear of being "challenged" by Chris.' They had to work in the kitchen until all hours, and they had to talk in whispers for fear of disturbing Chris and Lori. 'It was always tense, people were always working on personal issues. It wasn't like a normal kitchen where people could relax and have a laugh', he adds.

Tony says that Lori Camm was Brain's sidekick and that she was constantly challenging the Homebase Team and Winnie about competition or sexuality or other issues. The idea was that Chris, the priest, was the ideal man and, Lori, unofficially the priestess and leader of women, was the ideal woman. They were the models to which others should aspire. 'To be honest', he says, 'Winnie seemed the most abused woman, she seemed an absolute prisoner in her own home.' Camm told one woman that all she could give to Brain, as a person, was her obedience and affection. Clearly she was Brain's confidante and many assumed that she was his mistress. Ingham says: 'They were very, very close. People had questions about their relationship but there was nothing to suggest that they had a full sexual relationship.' He recalls one occasion as Camm left the room when Brain said: 'Isn't she gorgeous? Isn't it amazing that I haven't f----d her?' Ingham was perplexed. On other occasions he said to Ingham: 'You think I've f----d her, don't you?'

Brain used communications systems as a manipulative tool within the Homebase Team. The phone number on his mobile phone was highly secret and he gave it out to trusted people as a sign that they were in the inner circle. Anyone phoning his church or home number would be fobbed off by a secretary. He made a big issue of using a notice board in the house for them to communicate with him on, then attacked people for being too formal in their notes. If they chatted to him they could be attacked for being too informal. Communications within the Homebase Team were highly problematic and, naturally, the team members would blame themselves for this.

Tony did, however, come across some examples of abusive behaviour. One day he came into the house to find Brain in the middle of attacking another member of the team. She was distraught and the moment Tony entered, Brain accused her of flirting with Tony. 'I'd barely walked into the room and he bludgeoned her into a psychological pulp, accusing her of being a flirt with me', he recalls. Brain was careful that other members of the community never witnessed the controlling and abusive methods that he used on the Homebase Team, although suggestions of it came through a number of people's dealings with them.

One night at 3am, Steve Williams received a phone call from Brain telling him that there was a crisis and that he had to come and sort it out. He arrived to find Brain with one of the Homebase women who, Brain said, had thrown herself at him. Williams' impression was that Brain had been giving the Homebase member a bollocking for several hours and says that it is possible that the situation initially was the opposite of what it appeared. Possibly the Homebase member had resisted Brain but, hours later he had convinced her that she was throwing herself at him. At any rate, the member admitted to Williams that she had thrown herself at Brain and was threatened with being removed from the Homebase Team. He was called in several times to deal with women supposedly trying to seduce Brain.

Williams was also regularly called in to sort out other problems within the Homebase Team. Usually it concerned disagreements between the women over 'competing' with each other. He says: 'They were desperate to be top of the pile. Brain probably projected this on to them but they will have been competing to survive.' He adds: 'They were all genuine people who have been screwed up in what could be seen as an abuse factory.' Brain appeared to have succeeded in creating a system in which they were isolated from each other as well as the rest of the community. It appears that they were completely isolated and dependent on Brain; completely powerless to leave or even to see him as an abuser. They were far more likely to see him as their saviour and themselves as the problem. If Brain could control his leaders at a distance, it seems likely that he could control those hand-picked women who were closest to him.

Claire (not her real name) recalls, on a rare visit to Brain's house, finding a member in an intense conversation with Brain one morning. The Homebase member was partly dressed and appeared completely humiliated by Brain's onslaught which surprised Claire. Through a mixture of flattery and aggression he was telling the woman that she could handle his sexuality. On another visit she was surprised to see a number of Homebase women scantily clad in provocative clothes as they went about the housework. They seemed ill at ease in their clothes. Claire also met another member one morning to go to the gym. The member was utterly distraught, having been confronted by Brain.

But to speak to outsiders about Homebase was considered an intrusion into Brain's privacy, so Claire was told nothing of what had happened.

Probably the most meaningful statement about the Homebase Team is their resonant silence. With the exception of Linelle, the former members that I have spoken to are clear that they are not silent to protect Brain, but because they can no longer entrust their lives into someone else's hands; trusting is something that they will have to relearn slowly, at their own pace.

6

The Priesting of the Revd Chris Brain, Techno-shaman

As Brain's ordination approached, the church authorities were bending over backwards to accommodate their golden boy, whose experiment was putting hundreds of young bums on seats in a decidedly inauspicious inner city location. The Bishop of Sheffield, David Lunn, was enthusiastic about the work of NOS and had helped them to find an Anglican liturgy in Latin. Robert Warren, soon to become the national officer for evangelism (part of an interdenominational world-wide movement of churches, known as the Decade of Evangelism), said of NOS: 'It is integrating a whole number of strands of Christianity, not into a meaningless stew, but into a rich whole which I firmly believe means that its significance is that of a prototype mass-culture church. Their impact is to bring into question what, and how, things are being done in the wider church.'

Brain had an audience with George Carey shortly before he was made Archbishop of Canterbury in 1990. Robert Warren had taken Brain down to the bishop's palace in Wells to meet Carey, because Brain's work was so innovative, successful and relevant to contemporary culture. Warren had told Carey that he thought Brain's contribution to the Anglican church was significant and Carey was excited by 'alternative worship'. Brain unpacked the NOS vision and Warren recalls that Carey was impressed by the vision and the articulate, pioneering young apologist. According to Brain, Carey said that he would like to see a NOS in every diocese.

In early 1991, Warren and Brain co-wrote an article in the influential *Anglicans for Renewal* magazine about the dangers of the charismatic renewal movement becoming an entrenched dogmatic constituency, rather than one that was open to dialogue with other traditions. In it they wrote of God's rejection of fundamentalism and abusive power structures. God's judgement, they predicted, 'will be about an authoritarianism that seeks to control others and keep them in a place of dependence on strong leaders.' It continues: 'It will be about a repressive attitude to human sexuality. It will be about the psychological damage done to individuals by some healing and deliverance practices. All these criticisms are about the abuse of power and the way the strong seek to control the weak.' NOS was then held up as offering a more open and healthy approach.

In fact, back in Sheffield, NOS was still completely in the grip of Brain's desire for power. Although he had withdrawn from the running of the church and Trust, he had instituted a system which was extremely good at controlling both the leaders and the membership. Once a week, on Sunday morning before the services, leaders were given a time slot in which they could raise issues which needed discussing. The structure, which Brain called 'See Me Systems', allowed minimal discussion and maximum control for Brain. Ingham, who was left in charge of the Trust was so anxious to get his weekly 20 minute 'window' right that he would get up at 3am and go to the offices to prepare for the meeting. 'We were supposed to recruit, train, "duplicate" but we had to consult him at each stage before a decision was made and we could only see him for a few minutes in a very structured way', Ingham says.

Ingham would write a script, rewrite it, rehearse it and time it, desperate to use his precious minutes to get Brain to agree to his proposal. The issues were forwarded to one of Brain's secretaries earlier in the week, including exactly how many minutes each issue would take. When Brain arrived with his secretaries Ingham would go in, Brain would say 'Go' and one secretary would take minutes, another operate the stop watch, whilst the third would hold up a card which gave an answer: 'Yes', 'No' or 'See Me' (which meant it was to be raised again at next week's See Me session). Brain sat there mute unless he 'gave his mind' if a more expansive response was needed.

Issues raised could be buying a new television, putting a new tape operator on the tapes team, or whether a member could apply for a job outside NOS. Ingham would explain that the person joining the team had been approved for the job by the pastoral department, the recruitment department and the personnel department and Brain's secretary would raise the appropriate card. Once the time had elapsed the stop watch secretary would say so and the next item on the agenda had to be started immediately. Ingham says: 'You'd sometimes get a plastic arse held up, which was the signal that you were arse licking.'

The only other variation, when the stopwatch and minutes were stopped, would be Brain giving Ingham a severe dressing down or giving his views over a design or theological issue. Ingham was in the uncomfortable position of being middle man between Brain and Trust workers who desperately needed to get permission over financial, employment or relationship decisions. 'Naturally I got the criticism, frustration and anger from others for decisions that weren't my own', Ingham recalls. It was impossible to keep things running efficiently with such systems and Ingham recalls Brain's frequent taunt: 'Can't you run this organisation without me?'

There were other abuses of the leadership during this time. On finding out that Ingham and his wife were due to have a baby, Brain instructed Steve Williams to call a meeting of the original Nairn Street Community and the leaders of NOS and the Trust. They all arrived at a room in St Thomas's Church not knowing what to expect. Steve Williams then started talking about the population explosion globally and the efficacy of modern contraceptive methods and went on to talk about the importance of commitment to the NOS vision and the possibility of losing one's place in leadership if this commitment waned. If they wanted children they had to consult the leadership, Williams explained. Sarah Collins recalls: 'We were bemused but no one dared point out that Brain had a child and we all knew that we would be refused if we wanted one.'

A couple of weeks later Ingham, somewhat sheepishly, phoned round to share the good news: he was going to be a father. But his position in the leadership was in jeopardy. Williams explains: 'Chris was worried that several key people would be unable to fulfil their NOS responsibilities if they had children. This took no account of people's natural longing for children and he badgered and coerced me to put heavy handed pressure on people, as a childless role model.' He adds: 'I was unhappy making this presentation because I was having to say the things that had been previously said to me and caused me hurt.'

The core leaders also testify to receiving a substantial amount of abuse in restaurants. Brain often invited leaders out for meals but, for women particularly, they had little appetite and it all ended in tears. When groups of leaders went out to restaurants the tension mounted before they sat down. Where to sit was a major dilemma; to sit by Brain could leave one open to an emotional outburst, to sit away from him could be interpreted as rejecting him . . . and lead to an emotional outburst. He always sat at the head of the table, like Christ at the last supper, and he often complained at having to do so. No one else would presume to sit there. When the menus arrived the leaders scanned them nervously, feigning interest and waiting for Brain to chose his meal. The second dilemma was over; they would all eat and drink whatever he was eating and drinking.

Once at a restaurant Moira decided to live dangerously. 'I ordered a Budweiser', she says. Unfortunately the rest had gone for a Mexican beer. The other leaders relaxed, confident of who was going to on the receiving end of that evening's verbal attack. Sure enough it was Moira. On the subject of food, Moira was more careful: 'What would you recommend Chris?' she normally said. On another occasion when the rest had ordered beer, Sarah Collins was foolish enough to feel like wine. 'I was accused of power building, of making a statement. I got bollocked as usual and he continued until I was in tears', Collins explains.

Hypersensitivity surrounded any behaviour that could be seen as a challenge to Brain or a statement of independence. Many people testify to reading books secretly, in case Brain was reading them or hadn't given them his seal of approval. Pastimes, habits, interests or clothes could be seen as some kind of statement. Greg, a leader involved in arts, had visited Manchester and come back feeling satisfied having bought some clothes, including a particularly natty pair of shoes. The next day he sauntered into the NOS offices in his spanking new footwear. The response of the leaders was muted: 'Er, aren't they a little like Chris's shoes? Do you think that you could be competing with him?.' The next day, Greg was despatched back to Manchester the next day to change his shoes.

In 1992, Brain was made a priest six months early following pressure from himself and the NOS leadership. The normal procedure of a curate ministering under an experienced vicar was also waived because it was felt that Brain had considerable pastoral experience and it was clear that NOS leaders were keen to have him working in NOS as quickly as possible. The NOS community needed a priest so that they could celebrate communion together, and Bishop David Lunn agreed to an accelerated ordination so long as Brain went on to complete the course and to attend the standard post ordination training course for newly ordained ministers afterwards. Despite this, fellow students noted less regular attendance after his ordination. Because NOS had limited control over the ordination service, which was taken by Lunn in Sheffield Cathedral, their preparations were not as exhaustive and detailed as for most of their projects. They did, however, have control over Brain's clerical dress for the service.

About six months earlier Brain decided that they needed to have a 'robes team', whose primary task was to find him the right robes for ordination. They met weekly for three months, made drawings, and sent Tony, the NOS stylist, to various clerical outfitters in Manchester and London. As usually happened with project teams, Brain listened to them, ignored their advice and then made his own decision. In the end he saw Robert de Niro's robe in the film *The Mission* and decided that that was the robe he had to have. The robes team couldn't find one like it and eventually approached Paramount Studios, who sent them the desired robe for the team to copy. After Brain's ordination, the robes team had to find appropriate robes for the other ministers, though according to Marion who set up the robes team: 'This wasn't considered nearly as important as the palaver trying to find Chris a snazzy robe that was just right for him.' However, the robes team metamorphosed into the 'ironing team' whose new function was to iron the robes ready for services.

In August 1992 Brain directed the planning and production of an outdoor worship event at Greenbelt Arts Festival, a Christian music, art, politics and theology festival based in Northamptonshire. NOS had staged their rave worship in a 'big top' circus tent at Greenbelt several years earlier but this was to be a major event on the main stage in front of 15,000 people. It was to be a sort of 'bomb in the back pocket' to the progressive Christian community which Greenbelt Festival attracts. Because Greenbelt had a heritage of radical artistic and political creativity, NOS viewed it askance as amateurish competition. With characteristic arrogance they viewed Greenbelt as a group of ageing hippies and they were determined to show them how it was done.

The service (or performance) was to be called *Passion in Global Chaos* and the preparations for it took months. They hired a warehouse and hundreds of thousands of pounds worth of equipment for rehearsals. The service was to reflect much of Brain's recent theological reading. The writings of theologian Hans Kung about the importance of creating language to communicate truth were a major influence, as was Jurgen Moltmann's emphasis on getting in touch with a divine passion to confront global ennui. As postmodernists, they rejected a purely rational approach to God and sought to teach people to worship with their whole selves. This included the intuitive, the feelings and the sexual. As Brain said at the time: 'You don't have to enter NOS and leave your bollocks outside.'

Brain wanted to use images (projections and computer generated film loops) and music to communicate in this 'universal language' that was beyond the rational, yet could be felt (and felt deeply) and intuitively understood by people. Hence terms like the Holy Spirit were interchangeable with 'life-force' or energy. Matthew Fox and his environmental theology, known as Creation Spirituality, was another theological influence. The service style was dubbed 'techno apocalyptic' and was to attempt to present the audience with enough passion and life-force to shake them out of their complacency and to confront them with the magnitude of the environmental crisis and what the creator would have them do about it. As Brain said after the service: 'The service was adopting a style or genre that we've called techno-apocalyptic. It's not meant to be dissected or analysed but rather communicates in the same way apocalyptic literature does, that is, visually, spectacularly and emotionally. Some of the content is intended to ride over people and give them a vision.'

The Trust went into overdrive preparing slides, incredibly complicated computer images, laser images, music, lyrics and liturgy for the event. There were scores of design meetings with the artistic elite bashing out the content of the service. Initially Jon Ingham was in charge of managing the project, with Brain directing it. However, Brain put impossible demands on Ingham and he was constantly accused of jeopardising the whole project by his consummate mismanagement. Despite Brain supposedly directing the event, Ingham and another leader, Moira, had to prepare the briefs for the artistic teams. Ingham and Moira could never get hold of Brain so they based their briefs on things he'd previously said. 'It was a matter of trying to divine what Chris wanted from nuances in conversations or minutes of previous meetings', Moira says. 'He'd go apeshit because we would make decisions about design, but he'd go apeshit if we left things open and didn't take decisions to get things done, saying that artists need clarity and closely structured briefs to work to', she says. If they managed to get a few minutes to ask his advice, Moira says it was no better: 'He'd tell us that he couldn't shit on demand, artists can't do that.'

Moira claims that 85% of her time and energy preparing for Greenbelt Festival was taken up with trying to communicate with Brain. As with all leadership in NOS she says: 'You had total responsibility but no power.' She was so tense about working closely with him that she claims she lost two stone in weight during this project: 'You could often tell which women were working with him by their weight.' In design meetings Ingham was attacked by Brain for seeking to build a power base, for poor organisation and then for organising things too tightly to allow people's creativity to come out. Ingham was known for arriving at meetings slightly late and Brain stated, partly as a joke, that if he were slightly late he would receive a 'bollocking', if he were more than five or so minutes late, it would be a public humiliation. In leadership meetings the tradition was that Brain would attack someone usually by shouting and swearing at them over their failures, there would be a pause, then everyone else would join in, building on Brain's points. Then they would get down to business.

Ingham says: 'The amazing thing was that I had agreed to Chris doing this because I thought it was part of my discipleship. I was proud to show others that I had put myself to death to the extent that I welcomed such attacks. We all believed Chris's behaviour was for our own good and that his abuse was costing him a great deal because of his love for us.'

No one dared disagree with Brain. He seemed to be deliberately unreasonable with his leaders as a way of testing their loyalty. He also appeared increasingly paranoid, constantly asking members of the inner core what other members were saying about him. He made sure that married couples rarely worked together in the same area, presumably so that they wouldn't discuss his behaviour together or unite against him. He was also brilliant at playing married couples off against each other by gaining the confidence of both partners and planting doubts about the other person. This behaviour wasn't limited to the preparations before Greenbelt but many testify to it being an extraordinarily difficult time because Brain was angry almost all the time.

Ingham was relieved of his post of managing the preparations and a team was brought in to do his job. Sarah Collins was made overall manager and three others were brought in to work as stage manager, technical manager and administration manager. These replacements had, henceforth, to bear the brunt of Brain's tantrums and outbursts. Whenever Brain walked into a room the atmosphere changed. All would stop what they were doing and look at him, fearful that not doing so would be interpreted as a slight, a slight which would merit a 'bollocking'. Everyone was frightened of him, worried about whether it was their turn to be verbally attacked. The fear was such that they didn't even consider discussing Brain's behaviour amongst themselves, or raising questions about how difficult he was to work with, or that he was often too busy to attend a scheduled meeting.

Over a hundred people were involved in the preparations and it was decided that the band needed expanding and musicians from the congregation were drafted in for the event. At this point several musicians who had been held at arms' length were invited in. One member remembers that Brain invited him to a meeting and explained that it was a liability allowing him and his rampant ego and his sexually exploitative nature anywhere near the band, but as long as he agreed to submit completely to Brain and Lori Camm, they would take a chance. He agreed and Brain told him that if he let him down it would be like Judas betraying Christ.

Paul, who had also been deliberately distanced from the band, was also approached to play bass. He was told that he would probably play in the performance but that Brain, who also played bass guitar, might want to take over on some tracks. During rehearsals, Paul had to find Brain before the band commenced playing each track to ask if he wanted to play or not. Usually he didn't, but if Paul played without consulting Brain he could find him glaring midway through the song and demanding to take over. In one rehearsal, Brain came up to Paul and whispered in his ear: 'You'll never be like me, give it up.' Paul wasn't taken aback, because prior to this in rehearsals for a service Brain had come up to him and said: 'I know you want to be like me but you never will be.'

During another rehearsal whilst Paul was playing, Brain walked up behind him and kicked him with full force up the backside. Paul asked why he had done this and Brain replied, laughing: 'I felt like you needed a kick up the arse.' Paul recalls: 'The thing is you'd never know if he was serious or if he was just having a laugh, because people always said that Chris was good at challenging people, at teaching them using humour.' Paul's reaction was to spend weeks asking himself what it was in his own life that needed sorting out. Why didn't he react to such abusive behaviour? 'At the time I didn't question his behaviour because I trusted him, I felt that he was personally so sorted out. He was a prophet, he was the head of something that was going to change the world and the Church, so therefore everything he said must have been right', he says. When he saw others on the rough end of Brain's irrational or violent outbursts, Paul also interpreted it as Brain challenging them.

Anita Hurding, one of the handful of NOS members who has remained loyal to Brain, presents a different view. Before joining the Greenbelt team, she says she was 'vortexed' by Brain into facing a number of issues in her life in an accelerated fashion. This was preparation for her work as a bikini clad dancer performing in front of 15,000. She concedes that it was stressful but says: 'The enormous personal cost of such work was acknowledged because NOS was a task-orientated, pioneering organisation.' She adds: 'To break the inertia, and to put the Church in the forefront of artistic and technological revolution, there was a huge cost, but we all accepted it.'

Tensions increased as the day approached. The band were always somewhat tense, because they had to tiptoe round Lori Camm who was in the band and who, as Brain's close associate, it was worthwhile treating with care and deference. All the departments working on the performance had long meetings. The band and dancers, for instance, met for twelve hours to discuss cues and where people should stand and move to at different times during the one hour show.

When the event finally took place it was a stunning performance which dominated the whole festival. It was supposedly a service and not a performance, but in a truly postmodern sense the boundaries blurred and it was hard to tell the difference. The lights, the vibrancy of the dancers, the weird ambient or deeply rhythmic music, the rap and the house-sized computer generated images were stunning. It was a perplexing, vibrant and passionate service with clear apocalyptic messages about the way of the Western world. It was partly a harrowing, somewhat histrionic, wake-up call about the planet, partly a celebration of life. When Lori Camm, heavily made-up, sinister and projected onto a massive screen, read the bible passage from Deuteronomy her words gradually became groans, then screams as if suffering from birth pains. She then started laughing deliriously. As an attempt to sum up the simultaneous agony and ecstasy of passion, it succeeded.

There were aspects of the service which the audience found disturbing. The use of erotic lyrics in worship ('Come inside me') raised eyebrows and the presence of black lycra bikini clad dancers caused knees to jerk. The handouts, which likened the 'postmodern Christians' to Buddhists in their embracing the void, caused theological consternation among some, including members of NOS who weren't involved in the service but who had been invited down. Ingham says that they had been given no prior information about the service.

For a few weeks the letter pages in church papers ran letters from supporters or denigrators of the event and Greenbelt Festival circulated a letter apologising for any embarrassment caused. The only other fallout from *Passion in Global Chaos* was for the members who had put in months of work on the project. Paul (who didn't play bass because an hour before the performance Brain decided to play) recalls Brain calling a meeting in which he slated their contributions: 'He said that what we did was lifeless, completely unnatural and that there was no passion or energy in it whatsoever.' He gave the band an ultimatum in which he said that they were not indispensable and that people were queuing up to join and that they had better sort themselves out. 'We'd been working three months planning it, and 15 or 16 hours a day, seven days a week working on it and to be told that it was shit was so destroying', he says.

On returning from Greenbelt, Brain told the leaders that NOS was to leave St Thomas's within six months and they needed to redesign the service to fit his new theology. With up to 600 attending services they had outgrown the building and they felt that theologically they were outgrowing the evangelical charismatic theology of St Thomas's. The Sheffield Diocese put in a great deal of effort trying to find them a new venue. Eventually NOS secured a lease with Sheffield For Health for the underground rotunda at the Ponds Forge sports complex at a cost of £35,000 per year. Stephen Lowe, the archdeacon, started negotiating with the Church Commissioners to set up NOS as an Extra Parochial Place primarily because Bishop Lunn and Lowe felt that NOS should be brought within accountable church structures. It was to be a sociological, rather than a geographical, parish and the first of its kind in the Anglican church.

Meanwhile, Brain and other members of the leadership team had visited Matthew Fox at a conference in Seattle in spring 1993. Fox's theology is both popular and controversial. Expelled from the Dominican Order, Fox's 'Creation Spirituality' is considered by some to be neo-paganism in Christian clothes. Others see it as offering a holistic Christian theology, which addresses the destruction of the planet, patriarchy and sexism in the church and the need for a new mysticism and as a reinvigorated ritual to communicate in postmodern society. Initially Brain seems to have been ambivalent about Fox's Creation Spirituality. He said in 1992 in *Anglicans for Renewal* magazine: 'The problem with Fox seems to be not so much what he says but what he leaves out. He is very hostile to any kind of hope for a Western Church built on a fall redemption theology, and seeks to replace it with a 'new creationist' paradigm. Whilst there is a desperate need to recover the creation traditions, Fox's apparent proposal that they should actually replace the redemption tradition is unacceptable because, for one thing, it dangerously belittles the reality of evil. What we need is a renewed vision of redemption that values both traditions and combines them holistically.'

Nevertheless, after Fox's lecture in Seattle Brain gave him a précis of the NOS vision, some press cuttings and a videotape of a NOS service and asked him to look at it because he felt that they were already doing many of the things that Fox was writing about in his books. Fox was intrigued and perused the NOS literature on his flight back to the Institute of Creation Centred Spirituality in San Francisco. Fox says: 'I'd just been fired by the Pope and had no major projects to work on. I said to my friends at the institute that if NOS was half as good as I thought it was going to be I was going to spend the rest of my life doing it in the USA.' He started making plans to visit NOS immediately.

As soon as Brain was ordained priest he threw himself into teaching NOS about Creation Spirituality and the new direction that he felt the church should take. Ingham recalls: 'He came back fully on the scene at this point and took over, he grabbed the service back and introduced Creation Spirituality, changed the art and the teaching completely.' Fox's interest in shamanism and the beliefs of indigenous tribes interested Brain, to the extent that NOS began to call service leaders techno-shaman. He was very critical of Augustinian teaching, which he believed stressed the fall of human nature rather than the more romantic concept of 'original blessing'. Patriarchy, hierarchy, moralism and sexism and the damaging and abusive outworking of these on the Western Church were all laid at Augustine's feet. The leaders and members were given the task of designing a new service based on Creation Spirituality ready for their move to the rotunda in Pond's Forge. The NOS theologians worked with clergy within the diocese and members of the Church of England's Liturgical Commission to create what was to be called the Planetary Mass.

Much of Brain's thinking was reflected in a chapter commissioned by George Carey, the Archbishop of Canterbury, and John Habgood, then the Archbishop of York, for *Treasures of the Field*, the Church of England's book for the Decade of Evangelism. His inclusion in this prestigious book was a mark of the Church's interest in and support of the Nine O'Clock Service. It is an impressive chapter and presents the evolving NOS vision forcefully and persuasively.

Brain writes in the introduction: 'Our postmodern era has been united by current technologies into an instantaneous 24-hour information world. In the West, there is a growing insistence that we must live in the present, with a plural and heterogeneous range of lifestyles and viewpoints. In this multi-faith, multi-cultural, chaotic, white noise society, the Church's language and dogma aren't heard, because the old ways of presenting them just do not work.' He continues explaining how the Nine O'Clock Service is responding to this: 'For the Nine O'Clock Service, co-operating in Christ's saving work means taking full responsibility for our planet. Denial of that responsibility means denial of the saving work of Christ and collusion with the growth of pollution, oppression and biocide. Salvation will mean putting humanity back together with itself and with creation, choosing life instead of death.'

Brain presented, 'the bludgeoning of media desensitisation, producing a culture of low self esteem', and the desperate need for passion to shake off this 'deadly inertia'. He explained that passion 'covers a spectrum from the rediscovery of our senses to the refusal to get used to injustice. It means greater play and savouring of life, but also a greater hatred of anything that devalues life, whether it's people's pain and loss, the state of the planet or destructive, immoral relationships.' He continues: 'The Nine O'Clock Service endeavours to offer a non-dogmatic, free choice, where guilt and repression are lesser motivators, and vision, life, freedom, justice, passion and excitement are real currency. Christian community in that context is a place where complacency is turned to compassion.'

The Church was both intrigued and excited by Brain's unfolding vision. Here surely was a prophetic voice in the wilderness of dwindling church attendance. Here was passion, integrity, relevance and holiness. Here was a man who could change things.

7

Sexual Ethics and the Planetary Mass

On the outside, it was an impressive glass and steel structure dead in the centre of Sheffield; a modern facade to a prestigious company or a theatre perhaps. Inside it were clinical tiles and rubber plants, damp people clutching sportbags, leaving the Ponds Forge Leisure Complex. Taking a left down the broad staircase, still in prosaic bright lit modernity, led to double doors emitting snatches of ambient sound.

A few steps further and into a different world, the world of primeval techno: darkness and druidic white-robed figures around an altar resembling a crescent moon coming out of partial eclipse with the sun, surrounded by a circle of pillars. When one's eyes have adjusted to the ultra violet light, hundreds of black clad figures peer out of the darkness swaying to the swirling, strangely ethereal breaths of ambient techno. The world outside has dissolved into synthesiser and computer-generated mysticism.

A disembodied voice floats on undulating ambient waves of sound. The hypnotic aural ebb and flow carries the hesitant, ponderous amplified voice 'sample' of theologian Thomas Berry. He says: 'One of the issues that we face is understanding the order of magnitude of change that's taking place in our times . . . if we don't get the proper order of magnitude then everything misses the point . . . at this period of the senozoid, the human comes after the long period of development, we come at the end, what is now turning out to be *the* end because shortly after humans come to exist on the planet humans begin to terminate the planet. Those waves upon waves of life expansion are now giving way to counterwaves of extinction, wave upon wave of extinction. The rainforests are being extinguished at an acre a second . . . and the rainforest may well be the most beautiful thing on the planet, it may be the most beautiful thing in the universe, and a person has to ask "What are we looking for in life?"' The voice is slowly extinguished and the tempo built up with synthetic snare and bass drum.

The crescendo builds, and the white-robed Revd Chris Brain, techno shaman, moves to the centre and says: 'Hello everyone, welcome to the Nine O'Clock Service at Ponds Forge in the Diocese of Sheffield, and to our Planetary Mass. The Planetary Mass is our weekly celebration of life and our joint ritual of celebration and repentance on behalf of our culture.' The bass line starts, the sound increases coming from all around. 'Here we seek to mourn the destruction that we have just heard of and to cultivate a compassion that feels in our own flesh the wounds inflicted on others and on the planet and to awaken to the incredible awe and beauty of our existence with God.'

The ethereal music continues. He continues, quoting theologian Jurgen Moltmann: 'Whether humanity has a future or whether it is going to become extinct in the next few centuries depends on our will to live and that means our absolute will for our one indivisible life. We have got used to death, at least to the death of other creatures and other people, and to get used to death is the beginning of lifelessness itself.' The music drifts seamlessly on and the liturgy starts: 'The Lord is here.' The congregation respond: 'His Spirit is with us.' The music takes off, soaring round the rotunda and the first song starts, led by the band; the congregation on their feet singing for all they're worth.

Minutes later, the music fades into reedy synthetic sounds and other-worldly choral chants and one of the team of robed techno shaman leads the community in 'body prayer', a sort of Christianised yoga, focusing on bringing together the bodily chakras with the spiritual absolution. The next song starts with a chunky rhythmic, industrial sound, and then comes the multi-decibel confession built into the song, but led by one of the ministers: 'Creator God, the source of all life, we confess our sin to you . . . we confess that as we've wanted more and more we have dominated and exploited your creation . . . we admit . . . that we are complicit in crucifying you by polluting the air and the sea, by destroying the forest, by starving the people of the third world.' The rhythmic confession is punctuated by staccato 'vocal stabs'. The song continues and then a rapper comes over the top giving it all he's got and gradually fades into a sample of an eastern voice wailing. Then Brain says: 'God who knows the equality of all people and the trap of false dreams, release and deliver you. Amen.' He fades into the sounds of running water and birdsong, and then it is time for the sacrament.

The artists had delivered. It is hard not to see the Planetary Mass as a work of corporate genius, it is truly postmodern religious art of the highest order. As worship, scores of visitors (and many members) testify to the integrity and depth of their experience. The television monitors and large projection screens accompany the music with visual narratives interwoven with the spoken or sampled words, sometimes to underscore a point, sometimes to juxtapose and to point up ironies. It was a seamless act of professionalism and creativity. It thrust the vision at you through all senses, whilst looking like neopagan, cyberspace with passion, depth and rhythm.

Behind this weekly celebration were hundreds of committed people who had spent their spare time setting up the event. One of NOS's boasts was that 98% of the congregation were involved in some form of ministry (and in Brain's clubland phrase, in this sense 'the posse was the priest') and it is events like the Planetary Mass that testify to the depth of the community's commitment. Members of the congregation worked selflessly behind the scenes preparing for the event with little recognition. There were about 15 teams of people working on it with up to 70 working from 5am on Sunday morning until 2am Monday morning. For special events people sometimes had to work through the night. Julian Shinn, who worked in the stage management team recalls: 'People were completely wrecked going to work on Monday mornings, but the commitment to the vision was such that they were happy to do it although sometimes it was hard to enjoy the service afterwards.'

The community's financial commitment to the service was also impressive. People gave sacrificially according to their means; one anonymous person loaned £117, 000 for the technical equipment needed to stage the Planetary Mass. It was loaned on the understanding that for every pound that the congregation raised to match it, the loan would become a gift. The belief in the vision was such that this person was willing to give £117,000, if the sum was matched.

Member's commitment to the vision was reflected in the finances in another way that probably had greater financial significance. The members of the fundraising team were proving highly successful at raising massive amounts of money from trusts and other external donors for specific projects. For the year ending 30 September 1994 they had raised £54,555 of gifts and over £60,000 in covenants. The Trust's income was £271,940; their assets were valued at nearly £150,000, without taking into consideration over £100,000 of the matching loan. For a church based organisation seeking to expand and develop the vision, the Trust had a remarkably high income — the logistics of funding such a complex, large scale technological operation made this a necessity.

From the point of view of a trust connected with a conventional church such funds may seem excessive to the point of decadence, but considering the scale and cost of NOS's weekly services and other special events they were working on a shoe string. The preparation for each service was akin to staging a multi-media rock concert or setting up a thoroughly professional rave in a basement. It is little wonder that each service cost thousands; what is more remarkable is that the costs were kept so low and that the funds to stage such an event continued for many years. But the costs were kept so low largely because congregation members were prepared to sacrifice massive amounts of time without recompense.

It was the vision which inspired such commitment. Although the move from St Thomas's and the theological shift away from a broadly charismatic view to a synthesis of charismatic, liberal, catholic and ecological theologies, had resulted in some members leaving, the vision was still inspiring the community as a whole. A Nine O'Clock Service handout, which was given to visitors, summed up the vision effectively: 'A Search for Postmodern Christianity; Healthy Religion and Healthy Spirituality', it explained that the NOS community began: 'Where was the hope, they asked, in a consumption-addicted culture that is bent on destroying the life-supporting systems of the earth? Where was the sense of the sacred in a secular, technology-driven society that treats its members as cogs in an industrial era machine? Where was the passion and compassion in the civilised world to work for justice for the poor, the oppressed, the disappearing species of the Earth?'

It explained that the NOS community were confronting the addictions and abuses of contemporary culture and moving away from patriarchal religious structures. 'As a church', it stated, 'they find themselves creating a new model for healthy interdependent Christian community and moving away from unhealthy models for religion that make people dependent. Rigid dogma, abusive power structures, clericalism and cults of personality all seem to encourage people to be dependent, and contribute to a disempowering condition called religious co-dependence.' The final irony was the line, 'power and responsibility in the community are shared among teams, who implement the varied and complex aspects of the mass.'

Such inspirational writing failed to attract hundreds of new people (numbers fell with the move to Ponds Forge, partly because members of St Thomas's stopped attending), possibly because they were doing as Brain would have wished. Perhaps they were using intuition, as well as intellect, to make a judgement on visiting the Planetary Mass, and came away uneasy or concerned by the odd behaviours, the uniformity of dress or(what some thought of) as a sense of the sinister about the place. Nevertheless, the production of the mass by the community was not insincere, manipulative PR. It *was* genuine; they believed in it and were willingly giving their lives to it. They couldn't see the ironies, although some members do recall moments of doubt. Yet to follow these inklings meant dropping the vision and questioning their leader. The two were entwined and they were passionately committed to the NOS ideals, and Brain appeared to be the man who was bringing these issues on to the Christian agenda.

Fear was another factor. The fear of Brain that the leaders felt, many of their team workers felt towards them. Many of the leaders were instructed by Brain to model their behaviour on him, and some did (although in a milder form). Ingham recalls a moment of decision in the early years while standing up to Brain over the workload of members and resisting putting on a club night in a Sheffield nightclub. He realised that he could leave NOS or comply, but to comply, he realised, meant that he was going to have to start abusing people. 'To my shame I did that', he says, 'I started abusing people by putting emotional pressure on them, by corralling them into jobs that they didn't want to do.' He was held by the vision (and his early 'picture' which hadn't yet been fulfilled), by fear of losing his friends, of being a personal failure (Brain told him that he saw him as a lonely old man on a park bench with a bottle of cider if he rejected his calling), and by wanting to leave NOS in a situation where it could run without him.

Ingham compensated for his decision by making sure that he worked as hard as anyone. If he was to expect back breaking commitment, his own, he realised, must be even greater. This commitment appeared as consummate professionalism. Everything was done to the very highest standards and attention was paid to the minutest details. Agendas, procedures, minutes, debriefings were expected. The management ethos was such that the highest levels of competence and dedication were expected. This professionalism was a testament to their commitment as well as a by-product of the fearful, guilt-inducing culture that was the Nine O'Clock Service community. It is also clear that without the determination, energy and directive leadership of Brain, the Planetary Mass would probably never have happened. It is arguable that without his ruthless single-minded commitment to the vision which (despite his all too apparent failings) appeared to inspire him, such a massive, complex, labour intensive, hi-tech operation would have been impossible.

But NOS was the opposite of the things it purported to be. It created dependency and was a rigid, dogmatic structure. Its help for the poor or the environment was less effective than that of many more conventional churches. Possibly Brain made an issue of the very practices that he was carrying out in the same way a salesman says, 'I'm not selling anything', as his opening line. It would make abuse and manipulation harder to recognise. The issues may have been live issues for him because they may have been major problems that he hadn't resolved or wouldn't face. Why face them when he could project them on to his congregation and get them to face them for him? If challenged he would always have a plausible answer ready. He justified giving little NOS money to environmental projects by saying that NOS's job was to challenge the culture which would lead to greater giving to such projects. They were prophets not workers.

The efforts of the NOS community were rewarded when, in November 1993, the long awaited visit from Matthew Fox occurred. He was their principal theological inspiration at this stage and Brain's reservations about his theology seemed to have disappeared by this point. Fox's theology largely centres on rediscovering ritual and mysticism in the modern world. He draws heavily on medieval Christian mystics and the shaman and healers of indigenous people, suggesting that the reason-centred Enlightenment and the institutionalisation of the Western church had cut it off from its mystical creation-centred roots. Fox rejects dualistic concepts of good and evil, and stresses what he calls 'original blessing' rather than original sin. He is ambivalent about the deity of Christ who, he believes, was a prophet pointing to the cosmic Christ, or God force (which Fox believes can be found in ancient Jewish wisdom traditions). Fox believes that Jesus is *a* son of God (in the sense that all people are) rather than the Son of God. Through mysticism and ritual he hopes that the materialistic, consumption addicts of the West, will get in touch with God within them and approach the planet with the awe and energy needed to halt the environmental apocalypse.

Fox was deeply impressed with the Planetary Mass. 'It was twice as good as I expected, they had invented a new language to communicate, which is exactly what I'd been writing about', he says. The hard work of the community also impressed him deeply: 'The commitment of these people was beautiful.' Having seen the Planetary Mass, he told them that the work they were involved in was the most important thing in the Western world and that it was worth sacrificing their lives for. As a community, a sense of their own significance had never been lacking but such a ringing endorsement from a world-renowned theologian can only have reinforced this perception. There were other endorsements of their work. Apart from Stephen Lowe, the Archdeacon of Sheffield and Professor John Rogerson, head of Biblical Studies at Sheffield University, scores of senior clergy and theologians were enthusiastic visitors. In addition, several major industrialists and charitable trusts had given large donations to their work.

By the time Fox returned to San Francisco, he had made it clear that he wanted to work more closely with Brain and the NOS community. He was excited and inspired by their work. Brain and several NOS leaders visited Fox's Institute for Creation Centred Spirituality in San Francisco weeks later. In January 1994, Fox returned to Sheffield for a week of lectures on Creation Spirituality as his links with Brain and the NOS community were consolidated.

Yet behind the public front and the increasingly high profile of NOS, things were still amiss. Brain had run into trouble with the Sheffield Diocese for not attending the post ordination training course, a compulsory course for new priests. According to Stephen Lowe, Brain only attended one session and Trevor Page, the course leader, wrote an official complaint to the bishop. Brain was reprimanded for his lack of attendance and told that he had to start the course again next September.

A couple of months before Fox's, visit Brain took the NOS leadership on a management training weekend at a diocesan retreat house. The course was to be run by two of Brain's fellow students from his ordination course who ran adult experiential learning courses, largely for businesses but sometimes for church groups. These included team building exercises, role play and lateral thinking exercises to improve people's self worth and to help them to cope with change. Normally, on these courses the interactions could be fairly intense, but on this weekend the leaders were confronted with an aggressive, close knit dysfunctional group. They were constantly rowing (though not with Brain), couldn't be open with each other, and couldn't complete many of the exercises. In effect, they didn't allow each other to exist.

According to Moira, by the end of the weekend both the facilitators were in tears because the NOS group accused them of not understanding their culture, of having a hidden agenda and of seeking to control them. Brain had also taken the results of the psychometric tests and other exercises and graded all the NOS members, using terms like sick, psychotic and dysfunctional to describe them. Brain and Lori Camm, in Brain's assessment, were the most well balanced and fully functioning. They did paintings of where they saw themselves spiritually and, interestingly, Brain's was of himself alone in Gethsemane, deserted by his disciples.

The course had, through no fault of the facilitators, failed at team building or developing self esteem in individuals. The net result was a team with an acute awareness of how dysfunctional they were, and individuals with a heightened sense of their worthlessness. There was no 'original blessing' here. As Moira says: 'Brain's conclusion was that the church was messed up because the leaders were; we were to blame; he told me that I needed professional help.' On returning to the NOS offices, Brain decided that their pictures and scores should be put up on the walls of the office. It appears that they were used to remind them of their 'issues', and put NOS leaders in their place.

Brain was also involved with a group of NOS members examining what a postmodern understanding of sexuality should be. They went for two weekends away. Brain said that he was trying to bring a healthy sense of sexuality back into what was normally considered the spiritual realm. It was, again, all part of the damage done by the intellect dominated Enlightenment. Possibly Fox's teaching also influenced him, since Fox is keen that sexuality is incorporated into a holistic Christian faith. Brain's agenda seems to have been twofold: he wanted people to get in touch with their sexual power and to use it to communicate with others; he was also interested in exploring the boundaries of fidelity and of finding ways for people to express their sexual feelings in a healthy way. This related as much to sworn celibates as it did to married couples, and although Brain's explorations in this area had been going on throughout his leadership of NOS, it hadn't been so openly put on the agenda for discussion. Nevertheless, Brain's abusive behaviour wasn't restricted to those who were considering sexual ethics.

Carol, who had no part in the sexual ethics discussions, was told that she had to express her sexuality as a way of learning to control it and making it wholesome. Brain told her that she had tremendous sexual power which she could use for God as a leader. He told her that she was on the doorstep of salvation and that to go through, she had to learn to express herself sexually. Whilst encouraging her to talk about her sexual fantasies he told her that her sexuality was her holiness. 'He was offering himself to me for that, he was whole sexually and he said he wanted to teach me how to become whole too', Carol recalls. She was invited to put Brain to bed on several occasions and recalls one occasion when he was lying in his boxer shorts and they were kissing each other and exploring each other's bodies without going as far as penetrative sex. 'He was on top of me, he was rough, he wasn't connecting with me as a human being and afterwards I felt like I had been treated like an object', she says.

As well as the idea that he was sexually healthy, and was the only person pure enough to help her, she was also made to feel that in some way she was special and was supporting him emotionally. He told her that as a child he'd been starved of affection and that he was lonely and needed affection so that he could carry on with the mission. If she had doubts over his behaviour she repressed them. Once Carol said that she wanted more respect from him and, according to Carol, Brain responded with a major 'bollocking' and said: 'I cannot believe that you are questioning my respect for you — if you can get respect anywhere, it is with me.' She now feels that she was recoiling at some of the more brutal things that were happening, but she was repressing these feelings, partly out of fear: 'I admit I loved him and wanted his tenderness and his affection at the time but I didn't for a minute question his integrity or his motives.'

Anita Hurding was involved in Brain's sexual ethics experiments and, contrary to the popular view, recalls that at one meeting of the Homebase Team, Steve Williams pointed out that Brain himself was a human being and was working these issues through and hadn't arrived yet. She also recalls that Williams said that any people that didn't feel comfortable with exploring the issues could leave. She explored intimacy with Brain, and is one of a handful of former NOS members who have remained loyal to him and who don't feel especially abused or manipulated. Hurding's view is that people refused to take responsibility for their own decisions, and that they have done so again by blaming Brain for abusing them. 'There was always a struggle to get people to think for themselves. Chris was always saying that we should work things out for ourselves but we wouldn't', she says.

She believes that many claim to have been abused by Brain, because NOS attracted damaged people and because Brain was a strong personality. 'Because he's such a charismatic, intense and intensely creative person, and, I believe, intensely full of God, he was so attractive; it was easy to mix up his personality with God in him', she says. In her sexual explorations with Brain, she concedes that sometimes they went further than she would have wished and that the next day she would say to him: 'Such and such that we did last night, we went too far.' For Hurding the boundaries were clear, if unorthodox: 'We were non-genital, the atmosphere was more post-coital than pre-coital. Being orgasmic was something that I saved for my husband.'

Although Hurding claims that Brain was never presented as the 'safe man' to her, the majority of people with whom he was sexually involved appear to have seen it as a form of sexual and spiritual healing in which Brain, as the non-sexist spiritual man, was helping them to grow sexually. According to Ingham, Brain was exploring physical intimacy or intermittently involved with most of the wives of the men in the leadership team (usually without the husbands' full knowledge) as well as scores of women in the congregation.

Through his reading about the sexual rituals of Tantric Buddhists he developed the idea that sexuality could be used to raise spiritual power. By stopping before orgasm during masturbation, Brain believed that immense sexual and spiritual power could be raised which they could use for God. This related to celibates too. Ingham recalls: 'Brain often used a book called *The Art of Sexual Ecstasy*, about Tantric sex, with many including celibate women, because he said that people that were celibate needed to express their sexual energy.' People were encouraged to masturbate as a way of developing the erotic, which as part of the human psyche, needed developing. He felt that this teaching was particularly relevant for celibates. Ingham adds: 'The idea was that if they didn't come, it increased their sexual energy which would help them become whole people. He also advised me to do this as a way of increasing my life-force.'

Sarah Collins, who attended both sexual ethics weekends, says that despite all the high flown theological talk, Brain's agenda had nothing to do with ethics and everything to do with sex. She sums up the feelings of many when she says: 'All the stuff about sexual ethics was just clever language; basically it was about one bloke getting his rocks off with about 40 women.'

It was a convincing smokescreen. Julian Shinn recalls that sometimes new members would question Brain's involvement with a team of beautiful women: 'I would explain to them that Chris had worked out his sexism and was on such a spiritual level that there wasn't a problem, that he was beyond the normal physical lusts that the rest of us struggled with. On one occasion, he overheard Brain telling Camm how she really turned him on as he watched her leading a Planetary Mass, and he thought to himself: 'Isn't it brilliant that he is so sexually sorted out that he can be that honest with women.' Another member relates that Brain implied that he was the only genuine, integrated non sexist male. He said to her : 'I am the only really heterosexual man.'

According to Suzanne (not her real name), some of this abusive behaviour was demonstrated by Steve Williams, one of Brain's key leaders. Years earlier Brain had asked her to join what was to become the Homebase Team but, following her rejection of his physical advances, she had been told that he couldn't trust her. Later, Suzanne was instructed to discuss celibacy with Steve Williams, her pastoral supervisor. She told Williams that she didn't feel that she was cut out for celibacy and, according to Suzanne, he told her that she could still have limited physical contact with someone that she could trust and who was close to God. Suzanne says: 'He said that kissing me was okay because he was getting nothing out of it. It was to be business-like, he was helping me develop my sexuality as a celibate and he said that I could trust him.' She adds: 'The idea was that to be a whole person you had to be sexual, and if you weren't a whole person you couldn't serve God, so celibates had to develop their sexual nature, it was seen as healthy.'

Suzanne claims that a blurring of the boundaries occurred over years, but particularly during a twelve month period, and culminated in her staying the night at Williams' house. She is clear that the physical contact with Williams was not mutual or romantic, and that she resisted it. She says things went much too far that night (but did not include sexual intercourse) and she told Williams that what he was doing was wrong and she only wanted to know him as a friend. Suzanne says that the reason she did not make a complaint was that she was so controlled and manipulated by her experiences within NOS, that she wanted to maintain the friendship, and because of this was concerned about Williams' personal and professional future. At the time, she thought that to leave NOS meant to lose out on God's plans for her life. After this point, Suzanne saw nothing of Williams again although when word got back to Brain some time later about the relationship, Williams stood down as NOS's pastoral leader. By this time, Suzanne had left NOS (convinced that she was going to burn in hell) with the support of newly found friends from outside the congregation.

For his part, Williams concedes that the boundaries blurred with Suzanne over a period of years and that he had limited sexual contact with her, but he claims that it was mutual and only happened once after which he refused to see her again. He denies that he attempted to persuade Suzanne to become celibate. He claims that prior to his sexual encounter with Suzanne he had been under intense pressure from Brain and Lori Camm who, on a weekend away, had psychologically bludgeoned him into admitting that he was gay and had unnatural feelings for members of his family. Williams says: 'This disorientated and disturbed me in relation to some of my closest relationships; it rocked the foundations of my understanding of myself.' He returned home in tears and found that his house had been wrecked by a burglar. He says: 'I rang the only person I felt I could trust, which was Suzanne. She stayed the night and things went too far, which I deeply regret.'

He says that many of the leaders were desperately lonely, because Brain had undermined their marriages to the extent that he was the most important person in both their lives. Williams explains that Brain played his partner off against him until communication became almost impossible. He also points out that boundaries were blurred, because of the emphasis on intimacy and expressing sexuality within NOS. He believes that after the NOS stories broke in the press, some women reinterpreted what at the time they had understood as mutual acts, as one-sided and abusive. He says: 'I admit that what went on was wrong but it was not that simple; in my view it was also two-sided.'

He says: 'I am deeply sorry for my part in the evident hurt caused to some people by the abuses of power that took place in the community, as I made clear publicly at the time that I left.' He adds: 'I too was one of those humiliated, neutered and abused but I also have to face my responsibility for negligence, for weakness and deliberate fault as well as acknowledging the systematic destruction of independence of mind and distortion of the vision of the Kingdom of God (for which I am not responsible) that has tainted us all.'

When Williams was sacked he faced a moment of decision, but because his marriage was breaking down and he was desperate to leave NOS and start anew, but he didn't take it. 'I knew that I had Chris by the short and curlies when he sacked me. The idea of him sacking me for sexual misconduct was bizarre', he says, adding: 'I could have blown the whistle, based on what I had worked out about his conduct, but I was more bothered about my own problems; I just wanted to get out.'

Not surprisingly, with the exploratory approach to sex within NOS and the previously established 'anti-couplism', there was a considerable amount of sexual and relational impropriety. Before and following the scandal some left their partners for others, some have split up with a degree of mutuality, some have worked through the consequences of the unfaithfulness and are still together. Others felt that Brain's control over them was such that they yielded to his suggestions of entering into relationships which weren't helpful. The norm at the time, however, was celibacy for single people close to Brain.

8

Coals to Newcastle, Cults to California

The end was nigh. It was inevitable that — with a leader abusing dozens of women, undermining the marriages of his leaders, emotionally and psychologically abusing those that had contact with him — the bubble was going to burst. He was a leader who demanded total control, but was largely unavailable to make decisions, who was subject to extreme irrational outbursts and unfounded suspicions of plots against him by his leaders. He could not sustain an organisation for long. It was straining at the seams and something had to give, and when it did, it was likely that the whole organisation would fall like a set of dominoes.

The first clear sign that things were not as they should be came from Mel Lloyd who, as early as autumn 1992, wrote to the Bishop of Sheffield complaining about the abuse of power in the NOS leadership, specifically saying that the leaders' approach to Brain was verging on idolatry and that there was a complete absence of democracy which led to severely abusive treatment of the members. The bishop met with Lloyd to discuss her concerns, but partly because Mel's letter included reference to prophecies that she had had concerning the demise of NOS, he was sceptical about its veracity. The NOS leadership, aware of Lloyd's letter, also took steps to limit the damage. Steve Williams wrote to the bishop explaining that Mel was mentally unstable due to a serious illness. The bishop discounted the letter as unreliable and took no further action.

However, some of the clergy were beginning to have reservations about NOS too. These concerns coincided with Brain deciding that he wanted a rest from leading the church. He approached Stephen Lowe in October 1993 saying that he needed a break; that he was burnt out owing to the strain of having set up the Planetary Mass and orchestrated the move to Ponds Forge. He proposed that Luke (not his real name), one of the leadership team, take over and this was agreed. By February 1994 Brain told the diocese that he was standing down as leader of NOS and Luke was left in charge.

Lowe says: 'I was mightily relieved. There was increasing evidence in September and October of what one might call, Chris's hyper-messianic qualities, and I was becoming increasingly uneasy and said to the bishop that I was worried that he was looking and sounding too much like someone playing Jesus.' He had shoulder length black hair, a grand pectoral cross and was surrounded by disciples. For years the congregation had been dubbed 'the 72' and the leaders around Brain were known as 'the twelve' (referring to Jesus sending out 72 people to preach and heal the sick, and to Jesus' twelve disciples) and this had been accepted, but Lowe was becoming more and more disturbed by the messianic aura around Brain. 'There was this feeling of Jesus and his disciples or Jesus surrounded by a bevy of women that was increasingly worrying, so when I told the bishop that he was standing down, I felt nothing but enthusiasm.' These and other concerns about NOS and Brain's effect on NOS were shortly due to proliferate.

However, Brain's explanations to his leaders of his standing down are interesting. He took Sarah Collins out in his car and told her that he was going to resign. He was crying for most of the journey, and said that he couldn't cope with the pressure of leading NOS, people were projecting their problems onto him and he felt that he was close to a nervous breakdown. She was puzzled and troubled, and after a long angst-ridden journey he dropped her off, asking her if she would stand by him if anything came out in the press about him. She had no idea what he meant and said so. He then said: 'My conscience is clear, Sarah, isn't it?' Sarah responded by saying: 'That's for you to know, Chris, I can't answer that.'

Possibly as retribution for this lack of affirmation, weeks later when Brain told the congregation that he was standing down and announced the new leadership team, she was not included. 'Nobody told me that I wasn't on it and I assumed that it was a mistake. When I found out I was furious at being dropped after giving years of my life without even being given an explanation', she says. It was probably no accident that before he stood down Brain sacked the old leaders, and put in their stead a younger more malleable group. Possibly he was worried about the first generation leaders' greater knowledge of him and his failings, possibly it was because he wanted a team that he could control more easily.

Brain's resignation speech also reflected a strange obsession with martyrdom. He stressed how hard the job was, what extreme circumstances he had struggled with to bring NOS to this point and apparently suggested that he had sacrificed himself for the congregation. 'His basic message was', Collins recalls, 'I've been taking on your shit and it's time for me to stop.' He also subtly criticised the old leaders and lauded the new ones in whom he suggested the congregation could place their trust, once he had left.

Brain's concern with martyrdom is confirmed by Steve Williams, who recalls Brain's interest in the media frenzy surrounding David Koresh and his Branch Davidian cult in Waco. According to Williams, Brain was fascinated and disturbed by David Koresh and his treatment by the media, and said: 'One day they're going to do this to me.' For years Brain had spoken of the persecution that would descend on NOS from outside but his emphasis appears to have shifted towards personal martyrdom and a sense of being deserted by his followers. Others in the leadership testify to his increasing paranoia during the later years.

Malcolm Schooling (who replaced Ingham as Brain's PA and general manager of the Trust) says that Brain was obsessive about his health. Although none of the leaders had ever seen Brain so much as wheeze, he was convinced that he had asthma and it was one of the PA's responsibilities to set his watch alarm to go off every four hours so that he could have his dose of Ventolin. Schooling also had to change Brain's bed sheets for him when travelling abroad, so that Brain wasn't affected by the dust particles in the linen. 'When travelling with Chris, it was like he took his whole medicine cabinet on tour', he recalls. He also blamed the other leaders for the fact that he was overweight, saying that the food they chose in restaurants made him unhealthy and made him feel so bad about his body that he didn't want to go to the gym. Schooling says: 'The irony was that we only ever went to restaurants with him, and everyone made sure to chose their food after him and was careful they ate the same food for fear of being accused of competing with him.'

During the final years other behaviour emerged, which appears to reflect an increasingly unstable mental condition. If male leaders were seen having independent contact with any of Brain's favoured women, they laid themselves open to being attacked and humiliated, accused of building a power base and being told not to see them alone in the future. At a conference in Ireland, Luke and Ingham were challenged about their sexuality and agreed that they were both partly gay (they see things differently now). Brain convinced Ingham that he was attracted to Brain and that he was constantly staring at his backside. Although it meant nothing to Ingham at the time, he accepted that Brain must be right: 'I've since found out that Brain had accused the women on Homebase of staring at my backside. He seems to have been threatened by my physique and tried to project that on to me.'

Brain's hyper-sensitivity was also threatened by noisy cereal crunching. 'One morning I was apparently eating my cereal noisily and Brain made it into a big issue and accused me of trying to dominate the group because of my rage at not being the most important person in the group', Ingham recalls ruefully. It was taken as evidence of trying to build a power base. The issue went on all day. More evidence of trying to dominate was urinating noisily in the water at the bottom of wall urinals rather than urinating against the ceramic walls.

This insecurity demonstrated itself on another occasion when he was at the gym with Luke. They went on a fitness testing machine. Brain scored seven and Luke scored nine. Brain couldn't believe that Luke's score bettered his own and insisted that Luke did the test again. He did and scored another nine at which point Brain said that the machine was obviously malfunctioning. Luke says: 'Somehow he rationalised my score down to six and, of course, I accepted it.'

It was on Brain's holiday, after he had formally resigned that some of his most strange behaviour occurred. The Brains holidayed with Lori Camm and members of the Homebase Team and John Ingham for two months in chalets in Gomera, in the Canary Islands. Ingham had mortgaged his house to pay half the cost of the holiday, which cost over £23,000, but nevertheless his role was to manage and not to relax. Relaxation was made impossible, because Brain insisted that Ingham play squash with him regularly. Indeed, Ingham recalls Brain telling him: 'You're only invited on to the court so that I can keep fit.' At the end of each game Ingham had to tell Brain what the score was, and that he had been beaten by Brain and by how many games, and who was the better squash player. If

Ingham won points by playing difficult shots Brain would turn on him and say: 'Don't put the ball there, it hurts my arm. It's only a game, it doesn't matter whether you win or lose.'

Ingham knew better. It did matter whether he won or lost, everything depended on him losing. 'He kept accusing me of being competitive and on one occasion when I won a point he confronted me eyeball to eyeball and said that I was leading him into sin because he wanted to hit me', Ingham recalls. Ingham worked tirelessly to lose every game and succeeded. Later he recalls finding a 'How to Play Squash' video in Brain's room and Brain came in, aggressively embarrassed, and said something along the lines of: 'I bet you think I've watched that don't you, well I haven't!'

On returning from holiday in the Canaries, Brain worked on a joint project with Matthew Fox to stage the Planetary Mass in San Francisco's Grace Cathedral. He spent a week or so in Sheffield before returning to the Canaries (at a NOS member's expense) for another, three week, holiday. By September, he was in San Francisco making preparations for the Grace Cathedral Mass with Ingham and a team of designers. The preparations took the usual NOS path of being meticulously and maniacally planned with a clear sense of how to manipulate the media and membership, whilst steering a steady path towards the desired outcome. In the minutes of a planning meeting from August 1994, discussions were recorded concerning how honest they should be with Fox's Institute of Creation Centred Spirituality and how they should lead the press. Also included were details of exactly how they should recruit NOS members from Sheffield to stage the mass.

The following stages were recommended:
'—just a warning (word in ear)
—chance we're hitting SF in October
—you don't want to miss out
—keep time clear
—make arrangements for time off work
—keep quiet about it.'

Fox joined the Anglican Episcopal Church of the USA to work with the NOS community on this and future projects and William Swing, the Bishop of Oakland, cleared the way for the mass to take place in Grace Cathedral. There were the usual intrigues and crises involved with NOS projects but the 35-member team set to the task with typical messianic zeal. A UK high street retailer paid for the equipment to be transported to San Francisco, and the show went ahead in November and received rave reviews in the West Coast US press. They had never seen anything like it.

Moira had unwillingly been pressurised into joining the San Francisco team. Before the project, she had been told that she was repressed and resistant to the vision, but Moira believes that Brain realised that he needed her to stage the mass successfully in San Francisco. Trust workers were sent round to persuade her to 'choose life'. Next came a meeting with Brain in which he asked her why she had become so negative. She linked it with a humiliating memory of Brain going too far physically with her, and her feeling of being physically invaded during the encounter. Brain explained that the feeling of humiliation must have originated in her past and prophesied that Moira had been humiliated and abused in her childhood. The blame for Moira's negativity was, thus, back on her.

She agreed to join the San Francisco project. The physical and psychological abuse continued during her involvement, but now she saw Brain as the solution, the liberator not the abuser. By the end of the project she was suicidal: 'The pressure had been too much, I couldn't cope with the intensity and the abuse involved in those kind of projects.' Once again Brain's involvement with Moira had left her taking the blame on herself.

On Christmas Eve 1994, the Brain family moved into Greengates, a £200,000 seventeenth century farmhouse in the Pennines given to the Nine O'Clock Trust by two senior members of the congregation. It had been worked on for six months at the expense of personal donations from people who were close to Brain before he was ready to move into it. The five bedroom house was refurbished to Brain's detailed specifications. Inside it was hi-tech Los Angeles style. Every room was floodlit and with fitted carpets or stylish floor tiles; there was a stainless steel spiral staircase and each room decorated in a different dramatic colour. Televisions were suspended from ceilings, four state-of-the-art ghettoblasters nestled between plants, paintings and objets d'art. Some of the windows were handmade stained glass 'morphic windows' in the shape of eggs or distorted ovals. One was at ground level looking out at cows grazing in a field behind the house.

There was a dressing room, playroom, bedrooms for Homebase members to stay in when they were on duty and a kitchen with stainless steel units and a tile floor. Outside across the courtyard a stable had been converted into a fully operational recording and rehearsal studio for musicians and dancers. Above the studio was Brain's library with computers, projectors and PA systems and a six foot high, 45 foot long window looking out over the Pennines.

Brain's annual expenditure at this stage was closer to an Archbishop's than a typical parish priest's. He was still receiving approximately £12,000 from committed members of the NOS community who were living the simple lifestyle to release him to pursue the vision. Some wealthy members were donating their savings or double mortgaging their houses to support him or the vision. He was benefiting from this to the tune of approximately two to three times the salary of many members of the congregation without taking into account approximately £600 per month expenses which the Trust paid for running his car, his cellular phone, and a research and development budget. Brain was still eating in restaurants, buying designer clothes and going out on shopping sprees. They were paid for on an Access card in his name, but it was not Brain who paid it off.

Although Brain's move out of leading NOS was welcomed by the Anglican hierarchy, who believed he was no longer significantly involved, it is clear that he found it almost impossible to drop the reins. By placing Luke as NOS's leader, Brain had chosen someone who he knew he could control and dominate. Luke's 'grooming process' for leadership is revealing. In the run-up to Christmas 1993 Brain spent months attacking Luke, telling him that he was the cause of all that was going wrong with the service. Luke says: 'Brain told me that I had become the Judas, that my repressed sexism was screwing up all the women and stopping them from growing spiritually, just by looking at them they were seeing my sexism and withering inside.' Luke went into a downward spiral after weeks of such stinging accusations, desperate to redeem himself and undo the effects of his sinfulness.

Then, one day after Christmas, Brain phoned Luke saying that he was desperate and needed his help. Luke arrived to find Brain groaning in pain with Camm standing beside him. Moments after Luke entered the room, in almost pantomime fashion, he said: 'My God, the pain's gone. Why do you think that is?' Camm said: 'It must be because Luke's the right person.' Then followed a Herculean prayer session till 4am when Luke left feeling that he had somehow done some good. At 6am, Brain phoned and invited him for a drive. On entering the car Brain said: 'Luke, would you consider doing my job?' Luke paused, then Brain said: 'I sensed in the Spirit that you're saying you will.'

Luke accepted and entered his training process as Brain's successor. 'I didn't know who I was; he had completely dismantled me', says Luke, adding: 'I was truly cult-f---ed. I was just glad to get myself off the hook and did the job for penance. I was willing to die to protect and help Chris and to build up the congregation that I thought I'd damaged so badly. Once Luke had accepted the job Brain constantly accused him of being an autocratic, egotistical, megalomaniac. Brain only had to give Luke a look to 'close him down'. Luke was leader in name only, he had minimal control over finances or congregational decisions or appointments. His real job was to inform and protect Brain. 'I was completely sucked in to a paranoid outlook, but I had to keep up appearances, I had to change things for the better and loyalty to Chris was the only way that I could see of doing that', he says.

Before handing over the reins, Brain went through the leaders and key congregation members with Luke, making files on them about the extent to which they had damaged Brain, or could do so in the future and the extent to which their 'projections' could jeopardise the work in San Francisco. All the people who were listed as dangerous, Luke now realises, had knowledge which could have exposed Brain's sexual activities and psychological abuse. Brain was constantly saying to Luke: 'Will Steve Williams betray me to the press?' Luke was bemused, having no idea what Brain was talking about. Brain was also convinced that his leaders were secretly betraying him. 'He was obsessed with Charles Manson, and even said that leaders thought that he was Charles Manson', Luke recalls.

Brain had also told Luke that he needed to make himself vulnerable with women, to lower his boundaries. He told him to choose a woman who he could confide in, explaining that he had to do this to sort out his sexism and misogyny otherwise NOS and its radical feminist vision would not survive. Luke says: 'He was trying to set me up to behave like him, he was trying to compromise me sexually and he more or less asked me to be physical with Winnie.' Then in San Francisco he told Luke that Luke's wife should be on the team to stay in San Francisco. 'I couldn't handle that. Our relationship was almost destroyed already. He was trying to destroy me and to completely control me, but I saw him as the answer not the problem', Luke says.

However, with Luke in charge there was a definite change in leadership style. He is a gentler, more democratic, more inclusive person. The change was largely on the surface, because Brain was secretly pulling the strings and Luke found it impossible to stand up to him. He attempted to base his leadership on the Chris Brain model. He was in a difficult situation partly because Brain was an impossible act to follow (and the congregation was devastated when Brain said that he was standing down) and because he simply couldn't do what Brain did as well — they were different personality types. Not surprisingly some of the abusive practices continued under Luke and the new leaders

Paul was asked to go for a drive with Luke one day when Luke turned up unexpectedly. They drove into the countryside and Paul told Luke that he needed a break from playing in the band. 'I was working a 70-hour week as well as 40 hours working for the band and my relationships were falling apart, I was cracking up', Paul says. According to Paul, Luke's response was to tell him that he was being 'avoidant' and he was using his tiredness to avoid facing issues in his life. 'The opposite was true, I desperately needed time to sort things out', Paul recalls. On another occasion, Paul says, when he asked Luke for time off Luke warned him against it by pointing to others who had taken that path and were now sidelined within NOS. 'It seemed a veiled threat of banishment from involvement in NOS with the implied fear that there was no life outside of NOS', Paul says.

Paul says that Luke's techniques were manipulative and reminiscent of Brain's practice. He says: 'I feel that in some ways Luke was as bad as Chris because he used his position and techniques learnt from Chris to further his own aims.' He adds: 'Chris may have designed the techniques but Luke swallowed them and from my perspective he had a choice about whether or not to continue with these ways of treating people.'

Luke's response to this is to ask what personal aims he was supposed to be furthering. He says that he was trying to hold the organisation together, whilst doing his best to meet people's needs within the congregation and had no desire to gain power for its own sake. He says: 'The crux of the matter is that the NOS system was abusive in some ways. I was committed to both the long term NOS vision and to the people living within it but because of the system of leadership that Brain had created the two were irreconcilable.' He admits putting unfair pressure on people to work for the vision but also points out that he pushed no one as hard as he pushed himself. He adds: 'Anyone comparing my behaviour with Chris Brain's must have had minimal contact with him; my intentions were genuine.'

Nevertheless, NOS was still an abusive and cult-like institution. Luke says that what he now sees as cult-like practices continued under his leadership and were sanctioned by him. If Brain or Camm said that someone was 'out of order' Luke wouldn't question this and would take the necessary steps to deal with them: 'On occasion I was arrogant and judgmental and urged false realities and people are naturally hurt and angry about that.' Luke, however, says he was not acting to gain power but to keep what he thought was right going. He says: 'Basically, I'm left as a focus for the anger of many in the congregation and I have to accept that is partly justified. But I was truly trying to hold things together in the only way that I felt I could; all the responsibility for NOS, for communicating with Chris and for lives falling apart was on my shoulders. The truth is I was on the verge of cracking up and if that sounds like a cop out, it's not.'

According to Ingham, Luke's trauma and isolation expressed itself in acts of self loathing: he mutilated himself with a glass and poured a kettle of boiling water on himself. Ingham says: 'Luke would never publicise his own struggles but he ended up in hospital twice, he was in a very bad way struggling to maintain the congregation.' Paul Hatton, a congregation member, also suggests that Luke has become a symbol for NOS and has thus become a scapegoat, and an object of hatred. 'When Luke was leader', he says, 'he was in a position of weakness and dependence; that is quite different from Brain's abuse of people.' He adds: 'I personally can't apportion blame to people who were so close to Brain. Luke is admitting blame (sometimes unnecessarily) rather than simply presenting himself as a victim.'

Yet the manipulation in NOS was not centred around particular personalities, it was a cultural dynamic, which appeared to have gained its own life. Former members tell of having their attempts to leave NOS discouraged by veiled references to the dangers of leaving the community and entering the world outside, of frequently being challenged about personal issues, motivations or hidden agendas. Fiona Thomson recalls: 'Powerplays and mind games were present within the leadership but they were extremely subtle. I believe it was connected with power and the need to control others'. She was told that her eye contact with on male leader meant that she was in need of affirmation as a woman who gave her personal power away to men too easily . Yet it appeared an attempt to gain power. Thomson says: 'The irony was that, it seemed, he was attempting to create the very dynamic that he said he was trying to remove'. The leaders were in a competitive, defensive culture in which power was all too easily abused and several members describe leaders becoming increasingly distant, supercilious and harsh. 'To resist or confront many leaders was a risky business,' Thomson says.

Despite Luke's easier relationship with Lowe and the Anglican authorities, some of the clergy were upset by what they saw taking place at the Planetary Mass. The Revd Dr Mark Stibbe who had worked with NOS when he was a curate at St Thomas's attended a Planetary Mass in October 1994 and was deeply troubled by the experience. The next day he wrote to Bishop Lunn voicing his concerns forcefully. Stibbe felt intuitively that disaster lay ahead based on the atmosphere and teaching in the service. He was concerned at an uncritical use of Fox's Creation Spirituality, and wrote that he felt that NOS were 'on the slippery slope towards neo-paganism'. He felt that the creation was being worshipped rather than the creator and was concerned that the congregation was teetering on the edge of an ancient heresy, Gnosticism — faith based on secret knowledge revealed to the elite, rather than revealed truth.

Stibbe was also troubled by what he saw as a hypnotic use of music and samples which he felt was more controlling than even the most directive and hysterical charismatic service. He said that the fact that NOS was being treated as a 'special case' meant that the diocese tended to give them greater freedom but suggested that their special status (as a church without a parish or Parochial Church Council) should require greater oversight rather than less. Stibbe says: 'It wasn't simply that I didn't like their theological direction, it was the whole feeling of the service and congregation that troubled me. I felt that many of the people that I had known seemed lost and confused, I thought that disaster was just round the corner and said so.'

To some extent Stibbe's complaints are those of an orthodox Christian from the evangelical wing of the church who is disturbed by a more liberal approach. Stibbe is a charismatic who was an enthusiastic exponent of John Wimber's signs and wonders teaching in his early involvement with NOS, and may have felt aggrieved that his teaching had been superseded by a more progressive, looser theology. Nevertheless Stibbe, who lectures in theology at Sheffield University, is no knee-jerking fundamentalist and his sense of an unaccountable church and an unhappy congregation was prescient.

Bishop Lunn wrote back acknowledging his letter and reassured him that the diocese was involved in overseeing NOS and was working with the Church Commissioners to bring them fully back into the Anglican Church. The archdeacon, Stephen Lowe, whose job it was to oversee the NOS congregation since their move to Ponds Forge in 1993, felt no such reservations. He was enthusiastic about Luke's leadership and what seemed to him an increasingly democratic congregation. He also attended a Planetary Mass in October 1994 at which he had been invited to celebrate communion for the first time. He was asked by a leader what he thought of the Planetary Mass and, speaking from a theologically liberal perspective, said to the congregation: 'Originally I was sent to keep my eyes open on you lot, to act as the bishop's policeman. But now I'm a complete convert to what you're doing here, your theology makes sense to me. Creation centred spirituality, the worship of the cosmic Christ is very much where I'm at spiritually. We're reading the same books.'

In November 1994, Robert Warren, who had left Sheffield and been appointed national officer for the Decade of Evangelism, met up with a former member of NOS. The member says that he told Warren that Brain had been having an affair with his wife (which didn't include full sex) and that he felt that others close to Brain may have been in similar situations. Warren has no memory of other people being mentioned in relation to involvement with Brain and says: 'I had felt for some time that something was not right within NOS, from fragmented and sometimes partial snippets that I'd been hearing since leaving Sheffield.' Because the information was passed on to him confidentially in a 'confessional' situation and because he had no responsibility for NOS, Warren took no action.

However Winnie Brain's mother, Shirley Stopford-Taylor, was more active in following up her concerns about NOS and the effect it appeared to have had on her daughter. She had been making investigations into NOS because she had increasing misgivings that it was cult-like. She felt that her daughter's personality had radically changed and that Winnie had lost all confidence and so she made extensive enquiries about the Nine O'Clock Service. Archdeacon Lowe got to hear about Winnie's mother's concerns. According to Stopford-Taylor, Lowe, then a regular attender at the Planetary Mass, passed on the concerns to Chris Brain, and phoned Mrs Stopford-Taylor and told her to write a letter of apology to Winnie and Chris Brain over her doubts about NOS. She wrote a letter but worded it so that it was clear that she was apologising for any hurt caused to them, rather than giving the impression that she had retracted her reservations about NOS. Lowe claims that he suggested writing a letter after a meeting with Stopford-Taylor (which she disputes) as a way of improving her relationship with Winnie.

Stephen Lowe then arranged for a meeting in December 1994 to seek to mediate between Winnie and her mother. They met but, according to Lowe, the problems were caused by issues to do with Winnie's relationship with her mother as well as her mother's sense that NOS was cult-like, and had a damaging effect on her daughter. Nevertheless, having had a meeting Lowe felt that he had done his duty. 'It was a difficult situation between Winnie and Shirley and all I could do was to try and facilitate an improved relationship, that was the main issue as I saw it', he says. 'The Nine O'Clock

Service, as a cult, was barely mentioned and, at the time, I believed that Brain was no longer involved in NOS and things seemed to be getting healthier and more democratic', he adds. Mrs Stopford-Taylor had misgivings about the meeting, but felt that she had done her best to make contact with her daughter. She says: 'The archdeacon strongly denied that it was a cult but time has proved me right.'

Meanwhile, Brain, Camm and Malcolm Schooling were busy going to and fro across the Atlantic in order to work with Fox and his Institute of Creation Centred Spirituality (ICCS). Brain intended to move to San Francisco with a team from Sheffield, and to work with Fox setting up a Creation Spirituality project using NOS's hi-tech rave worship. Fox provided the theology and the backing of ICCS, and Brain was to bring over the expertise and the practitioners who were already reinventing ritual and creating postmodern worship in Sheffield. The worship and ritual experiment was to be called The Ritual Centre and Schooling believes Brain was planning to take over an organisation known as Friends of Creation Spirituality.

According to Malcolm Schooling, Brain was adept at manipulating Fox and his staff at ICCS. He says: 'Brain constantly hammered Fox for being a guru, a controlling figurehead; within months he had taken control of Fox's lecturing schedule.' Brain would advise Fox on what lectures to do and what to speak on. 'Fox was so keen to help and said that he'd allow Chris to advise him on what he should do', he adds.

With the benefit of hindsight, Fox agrees that Brain was beginning to manipulate them. Brain had a hundred people signed up to join a community and Fox wondered why things were taking so long to start. He now realises: 'He had to be in complete control before he was going to invite the Americans in.' According to Fox, Brain also intercepted his mail to make sure that he didn't link up with other alternative worship groups in the UK. He says: 'Part of the manipulation of Chris Brain was that he didn't inform me of other groups doing this . . . He'd actually intercepted my mail and, in effect, forbade me from seeing this information.'

At the time, Fox had some reservations about Brain. On one occasion he felt that Brain's attitude towards a ritual was inappropriate. 'Once we'd prayed with the sacred pipe', he says, 'and I really felt that he didn't treat it in a prayerful way.' He also noticed that Brain never washed up or made meals and his lifestyle seemed incongruous with a spiritual approach to life. Fox says: 'He always had the latest electronic equipment and I asked people where did he get his money? That was a real issue because he claimed to be a street person . . . when I learned that an anonymous donor was giving tens of thousands of pounds per year that explained it and it's shocking.'

Brain's behaviour in San Francisco was bizarre. Perhaps lacking the three secretaries necessary to operate 'See Me Systems', Brain took comfort in his modem. Whilst living in a house with Schooling, Brain would communicate to Schooling in the next room using e-mail. Schooling had to e-mail him back; opening the door and having a chat was unacceptable. Schooling now sees this as Brain replacing his Sheffield control tools, his car and mobile phone, with a modem. He says: 'It seems insane behaviour but it was also more sinister, thought out and controlling behaviour.' Brain, he feels, was using technology to avoid discussion and minimise contact, thereby lessening Schooling's influence. What is more perplexing is that Brain told Schooling that he felt that they should communicate by e-mail rather than talking because it would increase their intimacy.

God had other ways of communicating. On another occasion in 1995, according to Schooling, Brain thought that God was speaking to him through the moon. This had started back in Sheffield when Brain had a mystical experience lying in his attic bedroom as the full moon had shone on to him as he lay on his bed. This influenced the design of the Planetary Mass altar, which resembled a crescent moon. One evening in San Francisco during a meeting this 'mystical vision' unfolded further. Brain went to the toilet and returned excitedly and later explained that whilst going to the loo he had felt as though he was experiencing a woman's period pains. Then Camm said that her period was just starting; a spooky coincidence they thought.

That evening Brain had another 'mystical' lunar experience whilst lying on his bed. He spoke to Fox about it, and Brain decided that the moon was chasing him and that this was God's way of telling him that his new phase of ministry should centre on women. The moon was a symbol of the feminine and of Mary,

Schooling explains, and Brain's sense of being chased by the moon was, Brain believed, simply God's way of confirming his plans to work with women on his new project. Schooling says that Brain also said the experiences were confirmation of the rightness of his relationship with Lori Camm. After his mystical vision Brain took Schooling and several of the San Francisco leaders into the mountains of Oakland. It was a magnificent clear night and they looked over the whole San Francisco bay area under a red full moon. Schooling recalls: 'Brain stood beneath the moon on top of the mountain and told us that God had called him to leave his messianic phase of ministry and to become a Mary figure, a leader of women.'

Schooling believes that there was method in Brain's apparent madness. 'He was obviously crazy if he really believed that the moon was chasing him but it was also a shrewd political move to set himself up as the head of the feminist leaning Creation Spirituality movement. By having this mystical experience he had empowered himself as the divinely appointed leader', he says. On returning to Sheffield, Brain took various leaders out to the lake at Greengates on another full moon and explained his new role. They performed a ritual in which they stood in a circle, taking it in turns to stand in the centre and receive blessings from around the circle. The person in the centre said a prayer to the moon goddess and released a pink balloon with their name on it.

In April 1995, Suzanne contacted Bishop Lunn complaining about abuse within NOS. She hadn't complained earlier because she had been recovering from her involvement with NOS. She met Bishop Lunn, who subsequently passed her on to Lowe. She told them that years earlier she had been subject to abusive behaviour from Steve Williams, a married man who had been the head of the pastoral department. She also claimed that, one evening at the Brains' house, Brain leant backwards into her lap and pulled her down towards him to attempt to kiss her. When asked what action she wanted taking, Suzanne said that she wanted NOS stopped, she thought that it was like a cult. Lowe reassured her saying that he knew what NOS was like, he attended most weeks. Suzanne countered saying: 'They're used to dealing with people like you; go and look in the corners and find out what's really going on.'

She also said that she was convinced that what had happened to her was symptomatic. She felt (but couldn't substantiate) that others within the congregation were involved in sexual misconduct. She told Lunn and Lowe about celibacy and the strange theology surrounding sexuality but believes that they weren't interested in hearing what she had to say, they were only interested in their showcase theological experiment. She asked whether Bishop Swing in San Francisco had been made aware of the allegations and Lowe agreed to give Suzanne his address but warned her about a possible legal action if she wasn't careful about what she said. Nevertheless, after meeting with Suzanne, the archdeacon asked Luke to find Chris Brain and to bring him to the archdeacon's house for an interview. 'This was a serious matter, we tried hard to get Suzanne to substantiate her suspicions but she said nothing specific. Although they were two years old, we took her hunches seriously and made efforts to try to find out what was really going on', Lowe says, adding: 'We were worried and actively looking out for further signs of abuse.'

At the time Brain was staying on the thirty-third floor of the Marriott Hotel, overlooking Times Square, New York. He was due to speak with Fox at a Transpersonal Conference. Then the message came through from Luke. 'It totally freaked him out and he became very reclusive. He only went to one conference session bar his own, and barely left his bedroom, let alone the hotel, during the whole week', Schooling recalls. Possibly, he could see the beginning of the end.

Brain returned and faced the music by explaining that if Suzanne thought that he wanted her to kiss him, she was mistaken. The archdeacon gave him a formal warning over compromising himself and others by putting himself in situations which could be misinterpreted. He was warned that the Sheffield Diocese would not be able to commend him to the San Francisco diocese if there was any further ambiguity. The allegations concerning Steve Williams were admitted and Brain explained that he had sacked Williams as leader. The archdeacon was furious at not having been informed about this event, and told them that it was their responsibility to do so. 'This was a flagrant breach of the procedures that the Church expected', he says.

Meanwhile, the democratisation process within NOS was moving on. Possibly owing to Luke's more approachable personality, possibly because of the more inclusive approach of Creation Spirituality, but certainly due to frustrations within the congregation, a growing number of members were unhappy about the NOS leadership structure and the fact that they had no influence on the decision making processes. Alan Gibson and Luke met and Gibson voiced these concerns. He says: 'There was quite a considerable feeling that although Chris Brain wasn't around he was still controlling things.' When dissenters confronted the leaders with their suspicion that Brain was still pulling the strings, it was always denied. Paul recalls a congregational meeting in which Luke said: 'I have absolutely nothing to do with Chris, he has no influence on me whatsoever or on any decisions made in the Nine O'Clock Service.'

Nevertheless, Luke agreed with Gibson to set up a democratically elected body in the form of a Parochial Church Council (PCC). This may have been one of his first genuinely independent decisions, certainly he was careful not to tell Brain about it. Gibson was given the task of leading a team to consult the congregation about how a PCC should work in NOS. Lowe had also been putting pressure on Luke to set up a PCC before NOS became the Church of England's first sociological parish, known as an Extra-Parochial Place. Gibson delivered his report to Luke in June and NOS was made an Extra-Parochial Place by Act of Parliament on 1 August 1995. Meanwhile Brain and others were only a fortnight away from moving to the Diocese of Oakland to pursue Brain's project in San Francisco. Within days NOS was to collapse around their ears and present the Church of England with one of its worst scandals in living memory.

9

Unearthing a Cult

July 1995 was the congregational break for NOS. During the break the bishop received a letter from a male member of the congregation complaining about the lack of accountability within NOS. Selima (not her real name), a member of the NOS staff team, had also sent a letter of resignation to Luke and fled. She had planned her exit carefully, changing her job and moving to a new address, concerned that she would be hounded by other NOS leaders, who, she felt, would put extreme psychological pressure on her to stay.

She had had enough of the abusive treatment that was an ongoing part of being a member of NOS, particularly for women. 'I was fed up with the bullying of the male members of the staff team and was concerned and angry that some of them were blurring boundaries sexually', she says. The men seemed, to Selima, to pull all the strings, to have all the power, and abuse it. She was also angry about the use of the congregation's money: 'I was concerned about the amount of NOS money that was being quietly transferred from NOS to Brain's project in San Francisco.

In a meeting with Lowe, Luke voiced his unease and sadness about Selima standing down and Lowe promised to see if he could help by contacting Selima. The archdeacon met with the member who had written the letter of complaint, and asked him if he could locate Selima as Lowe was anxious to get to the bottom of the reasons for her resignation. Meanwhile, a Planetary Mass was held on 6 August and a teaching service on 13 August. The bishop and archdeacon had taken 13 NOS leaders on a training course about the Church of England as part of their induction, since NOS had been made the Church of England's first Extra-Parochial Place. They were impressed with the enthusiasm and commitment of the NOS team.

Meanwhile, Selima had heard of the unrest of three other NOS women: Claire and Marion and Sarah Collins. Claire had realised that the Brain method of spirituality and self fulfilment was deeply damaging. Although she had previously had reservations about Brain and had found him disturbing, her loyalty to the NOS vision had sustained her. Earlier, whilst in San Francisco, Brain and some of his leaders had told her she should drop her friends and develop intimacy with others who were close to Brain. Despite the fact that she was married, Brain had also said that her wholeness and healing would only come through seducing him. She says: 'The idea of seducing Brain was utterly abhorrent.'

It was such events that reminded Claire of how sexually predatory Brain had been in the early years. At the time she was led to believe that he had curbed his appetites but in San Francisco she realised that he hadn't changed his ways, he was just covering them. By Christmas 1994, she realised that she was sitting on a time bomb. Whilst she was on holiday in July, she realised that abusive practices were probably widespread and that they had to be stopped.

Claire decided to talk with her friends about her feelings and experiences with Brain. They told similar tales of manipulation and abuse. Marion says: 'I realised that if anything was a woman's issue, it was this. We had to see it through even if it meant undermining what we had been giving our lives to for years.' When Selima spoke to Claire and Collins, they shared their perceptions and Selima decided to tell Lowe the substance of their conversation at her meeting with him that afternoon.

Selima met Lowe in a pub in Sheffield on Tuesday 15 August. She informed Lowe of the secretive Homebase Team, and suggested that there had been substantial abuse of power for years and was aware of an example of sexual impropriety involving Chris Brain. Power and the abuse of power were central to the Nine O'Clock Service, she said. It was a sham, a grand elaborate facade.

Lowe immediately called a meeting that afternoon of as many leaders as could be contacted at the NOS offices (known as the co-op) in Crookes. He confronted them with the allegations of abuse of power and long term sexual impropriety, seeking to find out more. He recalls: 'There was a clear sense of relief that the unspeakable had been spoken and as I went round asking them they agreed that something was very wrong with NOS and Brain seemed to be the common denominator.' Yet, it was also clear that few of them had a clear picture of what had been going on. Lowe then interviewed several leaders and something of the scale and nature of the abuse began to dawn on him. This was no Randy Vicar story.

Lowe then reported the allegations to the bishop, stating that Brain appeared to have been involved in improper sexual relations with female members of the congregation for a number of years. Lowe was despatched with an area dean, Peter Craig-Wild to visit Brain at Greengate that evening. According to Craig-Wild, when they arrived he had the impression that a NOS member was phoning Brain warning him of the nature of the allegations. His first impressions were of the lavish surroundings at Greengate; it seemed incongruous for a priest to be living in such a house.

On confronting Brain with the allegations of sexual misconduct with about 20 women, Lowe was angry. According to Lowe, Brain didn't bat an eyelid at the figure and Lowe immediately realised that he had underestimated. He was angry about the people that had been damaged, and Lowe felt that he'd been betrayed, particularly since he'd spoken to Brain about Suzanne's allegations months earlier. Craig-Wild's impressions of Brain were primarily to do with the fact that Brain didn't deny the allegations, but neither would he admit them. Craig-Wild sought to pin him down and Brain was evasive: 'He gave the impression that he was admitting the allegations without actually saying so.' Craig-Wild made another significant observation: 'But the thing that Brain seemed particularly shocked about was not that the allegations were so scandalous but that somebody had told on him; he just could not believe or understand it.'

Craig-Wild was fascinated and disturbed by Brain's behaviour. He confronted Brain about his apparent lack of remorse and Brain said: 'Oh no, I'm really, really repentant.' Lowe told Brain that his move to San Francisco and the Oakland Diocese was all over and formally suspended him from any further ministry in the Church of England. Brain kept bringing the conversation back to his planned move to San Francisco, but Lowe was adamant that the Bishop of Oakland would be fully informed and that he could not work there as an Anglican priest.

By Wednesday, the leadership team had resigned en masse. This was partly due to the stress of the church falling around their ears, and the personal trauma that they were going through as the allegations came out. It was also because they realised that the NOS system was rotten to the core, and although Brain was the main object of anger, their involvement in holding responsibilities within the NOS system, meant that they could no longer represent a community which felt so hurt by it. Many members of the community felt that they couldn't trust the leaders.

On Thursday evening, NOS members gathered at the NOS offices known as the co-op. By then everyone had some idea of what was happening, but as they came together and swapped stories, the information that they were being presented with and the intensity of people's reactions to this meant that it was akin to a corporate deprogramming session. Within two days it was clear to Lowe that Brain had been involved in improper sexual activities with many more than twenty women. Lowe was in a difficult position because whilst he didn't want to breach confidentiality of the counselling, he had to ascertain the scale of abuse and sexual impropriety. He insisted that counsellors reported instances of sexual impropriety to him so that he could gauge the extent of it. He says: 'After the initial press release of 20 women alleging sexual impropriety with Brain, reports from counsellors kept pouring in.' He adds: 'The majority of the women who went through the co-op seemed to have been sexually involved with Brain.' After two or three weeks the diocese's estimate was at least two or three times higher than the original estimate of 20.

According to Pete (who as a nurse and NOS member was helping co-ordinate the counselling), there was a sort of group breakdown at the co-op as individuals realised what had really been going on. He says: 'In all my experience as a nurse I'd never seen anything like it; people were passing out or collapsing in tears; the whole community went into shock.' The Revd Andrew Teale, who was brought in to support victims, says: 'What made me realise that NOS was cult-like was the sense of two worlds or realities meeting head on, and as NOS reality met normality it simply collapsed.' There was an apocalyptic battle going on as people who realised what had happened to them set about trying to convince others who were disbelieving or in shock. A little later their energy seemed to vanish, as they collapsed internally.

At this stage, some of the leaders close to Brain were still convinced of his innocence. It was a slow dawning for some of those in the inner circle — for a few there was no dawn. Christine, who was on the Homebase Team, received a phone call in which Brain said: 'You're going to have to start lying through your teeth from now on.' She was loyal but confused at this stage. Loyal members found Brain a safe house in the Peak District and found him a lawyer.

Malcolm Schooling, who had spent much of his time in San Francisco with Brain, didn't hear about the allegations until later in the week and when he met Brain on Friday Brain pretended to know nothing substantial about them. 'During the week I'd seen him shrink to about half his size. He was constantly crying and looking forlorn and claiming not to know what the allegations were, and saying that the congregation must have gone mad', Schooling recalls. They met in a field and Schooling told Brain and his wife and Lori Camm that Brain was accused of extensive abuse and sexual impropriety. They all denied knowing what the allegations were and appeared to put on a completely convincing act of shocked and forlorn disbelief. Brain, in a sudden rediscovery of redemptive theology, started saying that maybe this would be good for NOS, perhaps he was the sacrifice that was needed for NOS to fulfil its vision and after ten years or so he'd get the credit he deserved. He stood with his arms outstretched and said: 'Maybe this is my crucifixion.'

On Friday, Jonathan Jennings, the Church of England's press officer, arrived in Sheffield. He advised them to organise some counselling for Brain and his family, to close the co-op and to say nothing to the press. Craig-Wild was given the job of liaising between Brain and the Church and he arranged to meet Brain at a carpark in Buxton, a small town in the Peak District on Saturday afternoon. He arrived feeling slightly panicky because he was ten minutes late. Brain asked Craig-Wild to come for a drive in Brain's car and as they left he said: 'I'm so glad it's you in this role.'

Craig-Wild believes that this was the beginning of Brain's attempts to manipulate him. Brain said to Craig-Wild that he should be unfrocked, putting Craig-Wild in a position of either agreeing or explaining that he couldn't advise on that. When Craig-Wild did the latter, Brain explained that he realised that he was ill, maybe a ten-year ban would work, he suggested. At one point Brain started crying and pulled into a conveniently situated lay-by. Craig-Wild says: 'This was part of the performance, one minute he was affirming me massively, the next he was trying to elicit compassion, to draw me in. His weeping was, in my view, manipulative.'

Craig-Wild believes that Brain spotted his strengths and weaknesses and started using them to manipulate him. 'He obviously registered my uneasiness in the role and my desire to do the job well and played on this, making me feel that I was in control and that he was helpless, but really he was directing me very subtly', he says. A psychotherapist came to see him with the brief of supporting Brain and monitoring his emotional and mental state and within days he started attempting to manipulate her. She says: 'To some extent we were all affected, we were operating within a situation unique in our personal and professional experience: the breakdown of a cult. Chris was now experiencing what he had always dreaded: abandonment by even his closest friends and allies; in effect, the total collapse of his world.' She adds: 'The situation was highly volatile and the outcome unpredictable.'

After Craig-Wild spoke to NOS members, he was given an insight into how Brain operated. Craig-Wild and Brain's psychotherapist started to recognise what he was doing, and both received professional supervision during their involvement with Brain, as well as debriefing together at the end of the day. Craig-Wild explains his own need for counselling and external supervision: 'To communicate with Brain I had to enter his reality, which was, in essence, unreality. I was worried that I might have taken some of his perceptions and machinations back into my life.'

From this point on he began to look for Brain's manipulations. On one occasion the Church authorities were trying to get Winnie and Ruth into a separate safe house, because they were uncertain about Brain's emotional state. The idea obviously appealed to Brain. He said to Winnie: 'It's so important that you get some space, you need it', adding in histrionic mode: 'If I have to walk the streets with a begging bowl to fund it, I'll do it.' The net result, according to Craig-Wild, was Winnie leaving but feeling highly dependent.

Craig-Wild set up situations in which he feigned stupidity to see how Brain would react. Brain reacted with anger and Craig-Wild apologised, at which point Brain hugged him, and affirmed him, telling him what a good job he was doing. He recalls: 'His affirmation was withdrawn then offered, withdrawn then offered; he deliberately put me in situations where I wanted his affirmation but I was made to feel that I had to earn it.' He adds: 'I realised that in a longer relationship with Chris it could easily get to the point where you'd do anything for his affirmation', he says. Strings were attached, but Craig-Wild and Brain's psychotherapist had seen them.

By this time, arrangements had been made for Brain to spend a fortnight at Cheadle Royal Psychiatric Hospital. The Church authorities had considered sending him to an Anglican retreat centre, but realised that they couldn't because untrained staff could not be left open to possible damage or manipulation at his hands. He needed professionals and the NHS had refused to take him on because of the difficulties of media intrusion. Craig-Wild knew that Brain was a convincing actor and was looking for him to start feigning a mental disorder to try to lessen his culpability. Then Brain phoned a NOS doctor and asked him about certain psychiatric conditions. The doctor refused to comment.

By Sunday, the NOS leaders went to Birmingham and Hull to escape what they realised would be a media frenzy once the story got out. Whirlow Grange retreat centre was made available for other NOS members to stay in for counselling and to shield them from the media. The stories of abuse were pouring in as scales were slowly lifted from members' eyes. According to Rachel Ross, the diocesan officer who co-ordinated the counselling, it was unfortunate that this all occurred in August when many of the counselling and psychiatric fraternity were holidaying. The counsellors (some trained, others clergy who were working as 'listeners') could barely cope and received counselling themselves. The stories that they were hearing tended to send the counsellors into an introspective tailspin as they questioned their own relationships and the extent to which they were exploitative or abusive.

Pete says that NOS members' trauma was such that some people were hitting themselves against walls and mutilating themselves. Rachel Ross believes that the trauma was so great because of the sexual, emotional and spiritual nature of the manipulation. 'It's hard for people to understand', she says, 'but this sort of trauma goes right to the heart of people's beings; it's also messy, it involves choices, mixed motives, guilt and complicity.' A spiritual vision (unlike political or business ones) seems both to be all encompassing in its scope, and to go right to the essence of people's identity.

On Monday a press release was issued saying that an 'internationally renowned theological and worship experiment in Sheffield appears to be gravely damaged after the uncovering of alleged improper sexual activity involving a former leader.' It continued by explaining that congregation members were receiving counselling and Lowe said that it would be tragic, 'if all that the Nine O'Clock Service stands for were to come to nothing because of its present difficulty.' It concluded with: 'It is perhaps too much to hope that those involved will be left in peace to rebuild their lives after such deep hurt.'

It *was* too much to hope. As NOS members and church officers prepared for the onslaught, all the national papers despatched reporters to Sheffield to seek out Brain and his victims to tell their stories. In the middle of the dog days of August, the papers had a very sexy story with serious repercussions for the Church. There was a media frenzy. It was front page news for weeks. It was also meat and drink to feature writers, colourfully unpacking this bold rave experiment and its consequences. Editorials were written under the legend 'Church of England in Crisis'. Evangelicals and charismatics (who placed the blame at the feet of Creation Spirituality and its rediscovery of eroticism) and liberals (who blamed the autocratic hierarchies of charismatic 'prophets') embarked on a theological mud-slinging match. Meanwhile victims found reporters on their doorsteps begging for sex stories.

The night before Brain was to be taken to Cheadle Royal Psychiatric Hospital, the press tracked him down to his bolt hole in Peak Forest and camped themselves outside. The Revd Andrew Teale was sent to pick him up. He was in a difficult position, because he had been involved in helping Brain's victims and yet felt that as a Christian he had to be civil to Brain. It was a fairly short journey but nevertheless Brain started trying to 'work' him. 'In the car he asked massively inappropriate questions about how NOS members were', Teale says, adding: 'He realised that I wasn't a confrontational person and he was trying to put me in a difficult position, to get what he could from me.'

Before Brain went into the hospital, Cheadle Royal made it clear that the psychiatric assessment would be confidential if the patient wished it to be so. Initially, Brain was happy with Craig-Wild speaking to his psychiatrist. However, Craig-Wild and Lowe were trying to persuade Brain to hold a press conference to defuse media interest and make selling an exclusive story to a newspaper impossible. Brain said he'd consider it so long as his psychiatrist felt that he was up to it. Brain then instructed his psychiatrist not to give any assessment to the Church of England on his mental condition. He then told Craig-Wild that his psychiatrist had told him that he shouldn't do the press conference. Craig-Wild says: 'It seems likely that Brain went off the idea of a press conference because it wouldn't suit him financially.' However, Craig-Wild made his own assessment of Brain's mental condition: 'I have not seen him show any genuine emotion in all my dealings with him.'

Weeks later, when Brain had left hospital, the Anglican authorities became aware of a press auction for Brain's story. Craig-Wild persuaded Brain not to accept a six figure sum from the *News of the World* because it was unethical and it might rebound on Brain if his victims sought to sue him for damages. Brain agreed. Two days later, though, Brain appeared exclusively in the *Mail on Sunday* giving his side of the story.

In it he said that he felt very guilty of abusing people's trust: 'To find that I am some kind of abuser of people I dearly love, in the areas I most passionately believe in, and thought I had worked so hard for, fills me with utter despair and I do not know what I can say. I am sorry for the consequences of what I have done. I can see what I could not see before and I am profoundly and desperately sorry.' He said that he did not have penetrative sex, and said that the Homebase 'handmaidens' were not slaves but were 'like any other vicarage, you always get ladies helping the vicar's wife.' Things started going wrong, he said, after his ordination, due to the pressure of NOS members and the Church establishment.

A keen sense of his own significance in the Anglican scheme of things comes through: 'I was the breakthrough for the church but it changed everything for me. Everyone became dependent on me.' The impression of Brain as a martyr came through more strongly when he said: 'I have no doubts about my faith. I have doubts about myself, whether I am suffering God's punishment or whether I am being crucified.' He continued in similar vein but suggested a new found liking for living simply: 'I find the idea of a simple life, with none of life's baggage, very attractive — on my own in the wilderness.'

The congregation reacted with anger at the article, which many felt was disingenuous and at times dishonest. The fact that it appeared to deliberately mislead, the fact that they felt that there were lies, the fact that he sounded as if he was surprised by his power and never wanted dependence, didn't encourage them to forgive him. A disclaimer stated: 'The *Mail on Sunday* made it clear that no payment would be made to Christopher Brain.'

There was also some consternation concerning the Diocese of Sheffield's finances when they announced that they simply hadn't the money to pay for the counselling of Brain's victims. Lowe asked a meeting of NOS members (there was no leadership to make the decision) if they would be able to pay and it was agreed that NOS funds would be used. Some time later NOS paid £40,000 for the counselling and administration of the crisis. They were also asked to pay the mobile phone costs for Lowe and Arnold, the Sheffield communications officer (this was later withdrawn).

Many NOS members were furious that the Church, which was in some part responsible for their minister's destructive behaviour, was unwilling to take financial responsibility for it (the diocese has since located over £10,000 which has been given to NOS counselling costs). To many of the former leaders, Brain's insistence that the Church authorities were seeking NOS money seemed to be coming true at the least appropriate time, with scores needing counselling, signed off work and trying to rebuild their lives. Many others feel that the diocese has worked sensitively and tirelessly to help the NOS victims and accept that the diocese simply didn't have the money to cover the costs. Gibson says: 'Stephen Lowe and many others worked tirelessly to sort out the counselling, to protect members and to deal with the press: they pulled out all the stops.'

Others within the membership pleaded with Lowe to contact 'cult experts', who would have the expertise to help people. Although there is a diocesan officer with responsibility for working with cult victims, he was never contacted. Luke says: 'We were strenuously trying to persuade the Church of England to get some counsellors with expertise in dealing with cult victims. It was the obvious thing to do but they didn't want to hear it; their denial was outrageous.' Brain's psychotherapist, who went on to counsel NOS survivors, says: 'Initially there was a feeling that to bring in specialist cult recovery counsellors might cause panic among counsellees but now it seems to me that by not explaining the damage in terms of cult dynamics we stopped people from understanding how they had been manipulated and left them, to some extent, blaming themselves.'

The refusal to acknowledge that NOS was a cult added to an increasing rift between members (particularly former leaders) of NOS and the Anglican establishment. It seemed to many congregation members that the Anglican Church was unwilling to use the word 'cult' because of the negative publicity that such an admission would create and this refusal appeared to sacrifice the care of NOS members. Lowe responds by saying that their main priority at the time was crisis counselling to cope with the extreme trauma. He adds: 'Had I really been attending a cult? It was open for public worship every Sunday; it's never quite so black and white as that.'

In September, Malcolm Schooling, acting as trustee of the Nine O'Clock Trust, went to visit Greengate (The Trust's property which Brain had been living in) with Jon Ingham. As they approached they were surprised to see a removals van with several men loading it. Immediately they realised that it was there at Brain's request (he still had keys to the property) and they were concerned that he could be taking equipment and furniture that didn't belong to him. They drove on and phoned the trust's solicitors. Schooling was instructed to go in as landlord and to check what Brain was doing.

They steeled themselves, walked in and immediately saw that Brain was taking things that belonged to the Trust and to individuals in the congregation. They told the removal men, who said that it wasn't their responsibility, they were simply working for Brain. At this point Brain and Camm came out of the house, furious that Schooling and Ingham had arrived and were attempting to stop things being taken. Schooling then phoned the police to tell them that a burglary was taking place. The police arrived and because the status of the house and contents was unclear (due to a legal dispute between the Trust and Brain's solicitors concerning whether they belonged to the Trust or to Brain), they said that they could do nothing unless they arrested them all. Schooling and Ingham agreed to this at which point the police phoned both solicitors.

The Trust solicitors said that they would have an injunction on the removals to Greengate within the hour, at which point the police spoke to the removal men who agreed to unload everything that Schooling told them to. By this time, Brain was trying everything to persuade Schooling and Ingham to let them go. He broke down in tears, tried to get friendly and asked them what effect their actions would have on Winnie. Clearly, he was no longer finding the 'simple life' quite so attractive. They were unmoved, and watched as musical instruments, sound equipment and furniture were unloaded and put back in the house. The police then advised both parties against returning to the property without getting permission from the solicitors. Ingham and Schooling returned to Sheffield, fraught but pleased with their day's work.

Simon Towlson, who 17 years earlier had bought the house in Parkers Road that the Brains had lived in prior to Greengate, was less fortunate. From the outset, the Brains had been on the title deeds as an expression of Towlson's idealistic belief in radical Christian community. In 1988, the house had needed roof repairs and Brain had told Towlson (through an intermediary) that they could only get a mortgage if Towlson agreed to take his name off the title deeds. He agreed in the expectation that he would be repaid when the house was sold. In October 1995 Brain sold the house, by then worth approximately £60,000. Towlson has received no money and it has been made clear to him that he will not receive any. He has regrets but nevertheless, his radical, Christian values are clearly still intact: 'It's no use ruing what's done, if one takes a long term view. We don't take our riches with us when we die.'

In November, days before a television documentary about the scandal, Brain resigned as a priest. The Church of England was pleased with his decision because it satisfied the NOS members' desire to have Brain unfrocked (although he was suspended from ministering, he was still technically an Anglican priest) and meant that they wouldn't have to investigate the complicated legal process of unfrocking him. Lowe said: 'We feel that Mr Brain has quite simply made the right decision for his own sake, for the good of the Church and in order to satisfy the demand for justice from members of the Nine O'Clock Service community.'

Six months on the community were busy repairing their lives. Many were still receiving counselling, some had left Sheffield to start anew, others were staying and approaching life with a new enthusiasm and sense of freedom. Some were keen that they should continue with some form of alternative worship. In March 1996, 40 former members attended an outdoor ritual in which NOS was symbolically put to death. NOS stickers, brochures, leaflets and documentation (including a Homebase task list) were set out on tables as people meditated and prayed. Then they were thrown on a fire. People then reminisced about NOS, took communion and set off fireworks. Lowe, who attended, says: 'Things were committed to flame to symbolise the burning of the bad in NOS and that out of the ashes something good will come.' Their first public service took place on Easter day 1996 at Hilltop Chapel, Sheffield, and in April a chaplain to the former members of the Nine O'Clock Service was appointed to help them consider what future direction they might take.

There is still great anger towards Brain and a suspicion that he can't help himself, and may seek to set up a similar group somewhere new. Elizabeth echoes the sentiments of many when she says: 'I feel as though I have been spiritually and emotionally raped by Chris Brain and the experience of being within a cult.' On hearing in February 1996 that Brain was setting up as a rave promoter in Los Angeles, former congregation members expressed amusement and concern. They are convinced that his need for power over people will reassert itself.

Moira stressed that he will need three things to achieve this: no publicity about his past, a team of organisers and money. Both the Anglican Church and the Creation Spirituality Movement will have nothing to do with him (Matthew Fox said: 'Brain gets an F grade for Creation Spirituality, he is not welcome in ICCF.') but members are convinced, with a mixture of anger and pity, that he will reinvent himself elsewhere. However, most people involved with NOS are too busy to give him much thought. One member tells of a dream in which she was walking along a street when Brain pulled up and offered her a lift. She said: 'I'd rather have a lift with the devil himself.' He looked up at her, smiled and said 'Have I ruined your life.?' To which she replied, 'No, you're not that important' and walked off into Boots to do some shopping.

Others who were on the periphery of the church tend to express less anger towards Brain as well as a greater sadness at the demise of NOS. John Chambers believes that despite Brain's clear culpability for some abuses within NOS, he is being scapegoated by a congregation feeling hurt and betrayed. He points out that

NOS was a task orientated organisation with clear, if massive, goals (reinventing the church) which demanded extreme commitment. 'It's no use joining the commandos and then complaining that there is bullying and that the officer shouts at you; we knew that our task was important and this was the context for the abuses of power within the organisation,' he says.

Chambers is also clear that without Brain, the remarkable achievements of NOS could not have happened. 'In ten years, the achievements of NOS were remarkable; there was no religious movement so relevant to urban culture or global realities, nothing tackling big issues head-on, or working at cutting edge art and community building,' he says. 'It may be a case' he adds, ' of a great man with great faults, but we must acknowledge both sides.' Chambers believes that to help the healing process for former members it is important to examine openly what went wrong and to what extent they are responsible or complicit in it, by acquiescing with an unsatisfactory system for so long. He adds, 'The same is true for Chris, for genuine growth and healing to occur, he is going to have the guts to face what he has done wrong and to admit it unambiguously.'

Kim Campbell, who had no personal relationship with Brain agrees that Brain's achievements and gifts must be recognised and is uneasy with the volte face that appears to have gone on amongst the former leaders and those NOS members who uncritically embraced the NOS culture. 'At the time' she says, 'criticisms of NOS would not be brooked, no matter how constructive the motive, our intention was taken as negative and destructive. Now exactly the same taboo operates in reverse and we're criticised for reflecting positively on our past experiences by the same people.' Campbell finds this disingenuous and believes that despite the revelations about Brain, the total rejection of the past and of Brain, lacks integrity because it avoids the complexities of people's motivations and involvement.

Ironically, Campbell says, Brain's dominant public message was about autonomy , equality with leaders and finding your own integrity. The reality of NOS was rather different. Campbell says 'In practice, however, a hierarchical system of strict accountability and control existed and if you sought to be independent or autonomous, you were disapproved of, censored and challenged about it.' She believes that the "denial" which made the gulf between theory and practice possible may help to explain the community's instantaneous reversal in their view of Brain in which he was transformed from Saint to Devil overnight. She adds: 'Whilst I understand how difficult it is to withstand the power of manipulation, I believe that the inevitable sense of self betrayal within this, has contributed to people simplistically demonizing Chris now.'

Campbell found being part of NOS empowering and inspiring and is keen to acknowledge the part that Brain played in this. She says 'I found that his teaching on gender relationships, equality and other issues, articulated much of what I felt with real insight and passion; the gap between his teaching and his ability to work it out in practice doesn't completely take away the impact that it had on me in establishing a framework for my faith.'

However, the best way to reflect the NOS community eight months after NOS's collapse is to let them speak for themselves:

Pete
'I joined NOS because I was attracted by the people. They were trendy but full of energy, hope and vision. It was the sense of community, of being part of a family all working together for a vision that we believed in, that was so good. I felt accepted for who I was in the early days. It was when I got deeper into NOS that the whole experience became addictive, controlling and damaging. I still have friends in NOS but the system that Brain orchestrated, has ruined most of these friendships.'

'In the long term, my experience of NOS was severely harmful. I felt inadequate, isolated, and trapped. I was made to feel that I was the problem, that I was abnormal, that I was malign and contagious. I attempted suicide three times. Ultimately, NOS was the destruction of me, for years it was as though I didn't have a life. People have asked why I didn't leave and there were several reasons why. One was that I had been told that if I left I would be punished and cast aside by God. Another reason was that I was inspired by the vision. I also felt that I couldn't leave my friends, some of whom were really struggling in NOS. The mental trauma that NOS encouraged was the worst aspect of it for me, but although the trauma and injustice in NOS has been psychological and sexual, it has also been a much more mundane abuse of people's commitment of time and money. And the commitment was genuine.'

'During my time in NOS, I gave money to the trust. I gave between £150 to £250 per month, as many others did. I was recruited into giving by Chris, who told me about the NOS 'vision' and told me what the money would be used for. Some of the money was used well. But in my opinion, most was not. I believed that my money was being used to build an inner city church with a calling to unchurched poor people. Phrases like 'feeding the poor', 'clothing people' and 'housing the homeless' were used by Chris.'

'Over eight years I gave about £30,000. I'm embarrassed to work out the actual amount. I feel deceived and ripped off and I know that many who gave to NOS or the Trust feel the same way. We did overtime, we worked hard to give (quite apart from the phenomenal amount of time that we gave to NOS). All the money seemed to go into the service, into styling and design. At the time I remember thinking that Sheffield's poor would be sickened by state-of-the-art techno-crap that we filled our church with. They would be humiliated by it; it was showing them what they hadn't got and never could have. But we were led to believe that we were meeting those people through the technology. We weren't.'

'We all lived as simply as we could so our money could be used to release people into ministry and to help people who had less than we did. A concern for justice was central to our giving. Now we have discovered that whilst we were eating tuna pasta at home, Chris was eating out at restaurants. It has become a joke to us, but it is a galling joke; our giving was shat on. Some wealthy people gave far more than normal people could, but it seems unfair that those that gave what little they had are left with nothing and if anyone gets money back from the trust I doubt that it will be the poorer donors who benefit.'

'When the scandal broke, I had suspicions that something was very wrong. I was still devastated and my first reaction to the disclosure was fury with Brain. I smashed my room up one night. As people talked at the co-op, it was like all the NOS taboos, rules and ways of behaving fell off me. I shared an apple with a woman leader and realised that hours before I wouldn't have dared, we would have been accused of flirting or of having issues behind that act of sharing. I realised that I had lost my life in NOS and I suddenly realised that I was free to be me. During that morning I went from cult reality to normality; but that process is still going on.'

I still believe in a caring God, a creator, but I'm not interested in Jesus or church. Church turns God into something abusive.'

Marion

'The day Chris was exposed it felt like I'd boarded a ghost-train I hadn't planned to ride; it had started and it was to late to get off. All I could do was shut my eyes and scream and hope that I survived. That went on for months, I barely slept, I needed the radio on through the nights to block out my mind. At first I was totally numb and busy; people wanted to talk, to find out what happened.'

'I still feel numb now, six months on. I'm back at work but permanently exhausted. Beneath the numbness is anger. I'm worried about what happens when it comes out, who I'll destroy, probably myself. I'm still in shock, my life for the last ten years exploded in August and it was me that helped load the dynamite and press the button. I feel like I destroyed something I created, like I murdered my own child but it had to be done because it had grown into a monster.'

'The NOS scandal wasn't to do with sex, it was about the abuse of power. But the Church of England doesn't close churches down if you complain that your leader seems power-crazed and psychologically abuses people. That makes me so angry. The Church would never have reacted if we'd gone to complain that NOS was a cult and Chris was a cult leader (people had complained for years, and been ignored). Of course if it's sex, then they react in 24 hours. So we were lucky that Chris got so careless and gave us such an obvious target — it wasn't so lucky for the women he was involved with.'

'I'm still extremely angry with the other leaders as well as Chris. Not so much with how they acted while we were in a cult, but for the way they have behaved since. They still act like they're an elite group and apologising is beneath them. Only one leader has said sorry but these people treated me as sub-human for years. They told me that I was negative, wrong, out of line. I spent years trying to work out what I was doing wrong, no one would see me socially because I was so unacceptable, not positive enough. I spent weeks crying, I wanted to die because I felt so alone and I thought I was going mad. The people who treated me like that are still walking around, I see them on the street and they smile and say hello like nothing ever happened.'

'I will never go near religion again. I think Christianity is a cult anyway. I now know how people can make you believe they are special and chosen by God and I'm sure that's how Christianity started. The whole way the Church is designed is to mess you up; you have to obey rules and be told how to live your life. You end up repressing your real feelings and opinions simply to be accepted.'

'I wasn't allowed to have children in NOS. I have a successful career but always felt that it was wrong, that I was selling out. Now I just want to try and pull together what I have left, maybe have a family and concentrate on my career, try and make friends with new people. That's as much as I can hope for.'

Alan Gibson

'Even though the last few months have provided answers to much that concerned and worried me about the way that NOS operated, I am left asking how it was that I and so many others were taken in so apparently easily. This book provides some answers but I still feel some embarrassment and cannot escape responsibility for not taking my own doubts more seriously. I still feel some resentment that there were people who knew just what was going on and chose to collaborate with the abuses, even to the extent of denying that which they knew to be true. My understanding of the impossible situation in which such people found themselves has grown (and along with that, my sympathy for them) but I am not yet at a place where I can unreservedly forgive.'

'The events of August 1995 left me first with feelings of release and freedom, followed by a sense of loss and major lack of motivation in my life. Over the months since then I have been through a variety of stages and, perhaps now I feel a desire not to see everything perish because of the corruption visited on many people. Some of the people who made up the NOS community do wish to stay together and develop a new identity as a worshipping community. I hope that we can enable that to happen; certainly we are encouraged by the support of the Diocese of Sheffield.'

'As far as my own faith is concerned, I find that my certainties are vastly outnumbered by uncertainties but this feels good and appropriate. Indeed I feel a growing wariness of those who claim to have answers and of any vestige of fundamentalism. I have many more questions now than I ever had about just who God is, about the nature and purpose of creation and I am happy with my lack of certitude. It does not feel easy to fit these uncertainties into a church and I find it very hard to envisage a church which does not exhibit evidence of misuse and abuse of power and authority.'

'It may be that what is left of NOS in Sheffield has the opportunity, once again, to redefine 'church', to tackle issues of power and of right relationships within a worshipping community and to continue, in a smaller way, to develop styles of worship which are appropriate to those involved, and still to do this within the Anglican Church. At the moment we are barely at the beginning of the process, most of our time is still being spent in picking up the pieces and sorting out the mess. What the future holds is unsure but what is sure is that it will not look like what we came to recognise as NOS.'

Claire

'Despite the sickness that Brain originated and that eventually destroyed NOS, looking back I have spent a large part of my life with many brilliant people. I have good memories of friends and fun, have experienced some real healing and have known times of almost tangible positive energy in worship. These are some of the reasons that I stayed so long.'

'It had taken at least a year for me to piece together enough of what Brain was really up to and to find the courage to say so. However, in standing against the continuance of the abuse, neither I nor anybody else realised the scale of what was being uncovered. After NOS blew, the first effects that I saw were friends that Brain had tried to separate, free to talk again. I also saw people starting to recover their identities. A lot of us were in shock and very vulnerable and our resources for each other were limited. Many relationships fragmented and the grapevine went wild with speculation and mistrust.'

'Since the scandal I've got in touch with a whole flood of memories of abuse and experienced extreme anger. I remember Brain's slander of people and some of his bizarre acting as he controlled and dominated group situations. I have heard horrific first hand accounts of how Brain conned, manipulated and abused people, invading their lives and personalities with his egotistical arrogance. I still don't believe that he is capable of genuine remorse.'

'I have wept over the amount of betrayal that there has been and I was profoundly disappointed by the lack of support from the Church, with some local exceptions. This was a blow to my faith. Some counselling made available by the Church was very valuable but the most significant help came when a friend paid for me to see a post-traumatic stress therapist who specialises in cults and abuse. She was able to say what I might expect in the aftermath and her predictions were accurate and helpful. One thing that she commented on was the violence of NOS terminology, which was peppered with phrases like 'getting hammered' and 'getting your head kicked in'— this aggressive treatment of people was developed and encouraged by Brain. If the Church had used cult experts I believe people would have benefited greatly but I suppose it was too contentious for them to admit that NOS had within it a full blown cult, having ordained its leader.'

'I am re-evaluating my spirituality and this is forcing it to grow and deepen but I think this will take a long time. It has been hard to stay in Sheffield around so much intensity and fragility. There's not the focus of the service to keep in contact with people but NOS is in the past and although I feel grief, I'm glad its blown. I'm pleased to see former members building their own futures. I'm free to try out new things and pick up old ambitions. A few NOS friendships have survived and I'm meeting up with old friends and family again. The barriers of NOS control are no longer there, which has given me back my freedom in relationships. So it's been hard going over the wreckage and there is more to reclaim but there is a new openness ahead and there is life, real life beyond NOS.'

Kim Campbell

'NOS enabled me to worship without feeling frustrated and stifled, at odds with those around me. It was the first time I could bring the whole of myself into a corporate expression of faith. NOS provided a complete context which was creatively rich, spiritually relevant and relationships which on a personal level were essentially healing. The language spoken was one I was deeply in accord with. I was inspired by the `vision' and passionate in my desire to work out in practice. I recognised there were problems, particularly in the way power operated and I went through a period of considerable anger and disquietude, but I made an active and informed choice to stay. The vision was empowering, and I believed we were on a journey which would eventually begin to address these issues. Ironically , the final decision to remain committed was taken just prior to the break up. I think the resulting sense of loss was made more profound as a result.'

'My initial reaction to the allegations was incomprehension, then shock and a kind of emotional paralysis. I felt sick at the extent of the problems. What followed was a sordid experience of a media barrage. The tabloids were on a blood hunt for salacious detail and the qualities were little better, printing the moralistic preaching of "experts".' The experience was devastating. I can honestly say that I felt more abused by the media during those first weeks than I had ever felt by any church. I was also angry with many former NOS members. I have no argument with those who suffered direct abuse, but many who had only the experience of an imperfect organisation also jumped on the band wagon. To be told by self-appointed experts that I was a deluded cult member, and implored by fellow community members to search my experience and understand how I too was abused, was really too much!'

'After the media barrage had died down and the initial shock had subsided, the overriding feeling was profound grief. Utter loss was sharpened by the general taboo against mourning the good. I lost a whole life context, not just a Sunday church service.'

'I guess that is where I am now. I feel utterly bereft of a context where I can freely express my faith. What remains is a binding relationship with God and a vision of how that relationship can be expressed in artistically rich, contemporary communities. There is also an utter lack of faith in people: the last year has been like an assault course training on the underbelly of human nature. NOS articulated a vision where the balance of power was restored to its rightful place and relationships of equality existed between ourselves and the rest of creation. The gap between this vision and the practice within NOS illustrates for me the fundamental problem we all have in dealing with power. I still don't know how we work that out in community. This is a challenge, which for me is right at the heart of my faith, but I don't know the answer and I don't know where to go from here. However, non-involvement is not an option.'

10

Church, Culture, Cult

On a beautiful Saturday morning 700 men are gathered in a Northampton girls' school hall. They are there for the sake of their masculinity, bonding with their brothers and calling on God to reaffirm their masculinity. Balding pates and baseball caps and close cropped heads are tilted back as they petition their Heavenly Father for shelter from the ravages of feminism, which they believe has marched from the workplace straight into church. The conference called *Men Alive For God* was organised by the Jesus Fellowship with the aim of helping men to find a role in what they consider to be a female dominated church. Women were barred from the meeting.

The meeting opened with a hi-tech light show and soft-rock style worship. A remarkable cross-section of males was present. From overwrought, lamely dressed professional types, to skinheads wearing leathers, jack boots and mohicans. All in the hall were singing, embracing and praising God. Others wore regulation Jesus Army issue in-your-face multicoloured combat gear with 'Jesus Army: Fighting For You' emblazoned on the epaulets. They looked like unshaven, warts-and-all-style Thunderbirds in their striking military uniforms. After a foot-stomping rendition of 'The Lord is a Warrior' chorus, Noel Stanton, the white haired and frail looking leader of the Jesus Fellowship, takes the microphone and chants: 'I'm a man, I'm a man, I'm a man, I'm a Holy Spirit man, I'm a winner!'

He goes on to say that church tradition has had a crippling effect on the Church, stopping it from reflecting Jesus' virility. As he shouts, 'Once women and kids went to church, now it's the men who are leading, we've got back to the biblical order', 700 brothers rise from their seats clapping and cheering. Stanton urges men to share their hopes and failures, to embrace each other. 'You must hug one another and get into the same bonding that the men of the New Testament days had', he says with the sort of whispered intensity that suggests life depends on it. He reaches an emotional crescendo, strutting, smiling, wisps of long white hair spread over his bald head, saying: 'We're men, *we're* the Glory of God, got it?

Women are the glory of men, it's in the bible. All men are biblically to take leadership, they are to be leaders.' He ends with a prayer, pledging that the men serve God faithfully as good husbands, fathers, leaders and disciples.

After the morning meeting Duncan Centamore, a mechanic and van driver, said that he'd been blessed: 'It's okay to be a man, I want to grow in my maleness, into leadership. After all we are made in the image of the glory of God.' He differentiated between life in church and life in the world outside. 'In day to day life equality is okay, but in things of the spirit it's different, men are ordained to lead.' Jim Redman, beaming in his combat style jacket and 'Jesus Revolution' T-shirt, also found the event helpful: 'We need to grow in stature, in self confidence; it's true men should be at the heart of church life but they've lost their place.'

The women had found their place in the Church: in the kitchen. A cheery, rosy-cheeked, Barbara Motherheart (her *virtue* name) explained: 'They need us to do the catering, we're really serving the saints today, it's a real pleasure.' Mick Haines, one of the afternoon's seminar leaders, confirmed this whilst explaining the contents of his 'Men needing to find their masculine role' seminar: 'There are a few women allowed in the building, otherwise we wouldn't eat.'

John Campbell, the Jesus Fellowship (aka Jesus Army) press officer, who organised the day, has another stab at elucidating the differences between the sexes: 'Men don't fit into church, they are ill at ease with the emotional aspects of worship and prayer which women tend to respond to.' Campbell hopes to demonstrate that there is room in church for what he sees as the more masculine qualities of boldness, integrity, leadership and decision making. 'The church is a place for action and ethics as well as emotion and compassion, we want men to realise this and get involved', he says. 'We believe that the main leadership should be men's but that there's room for women in leadership, underneath the men', he adds.

Depending on one's point of view, that male jamboree in Northampton could have been either a sinister cult involved in brainwashing or a fringe charismatic church, quaintly propagating a reactionary doctrine against the tide of history. One's reaction could either be shocked outrage or outright amusement. But the issue of perception is at the heart of understanding new religious movements or cults. It is even present in the nomenclature: *cults* is generally used by those cultwatch organisations who react strongly and negatively towards such organisations; *new religious movements* is the term used by academics who seek to take a less 'value laden' approach, but whose critics say they are too laissez faire.

The issue of perception was at the heart of the row between Home Secretary Michael Howard and the judiciary in November 1995 over whether the Revd Sun Yung Moon, the leader of the Unification Church (or Moonies) should be allowed into the country. The judiciary stated that Howard's exclusion order was illegal but he decided to ignore this and to leave the exclusion order in place. The papers lionised him because he was barring the leader of a 'sinister cult which sought to brainwash our young people.' A liberal minority complained that this was blatant religious intolerance, after all what made one religion acceptable and another sinister?

Indeed, one of Britain's leading academics involved in researching New Religious Movements, Eileen Barker of the London School of Economics, believes that the Moonies have much to offer converts and that they have frequently been unfairly treated by the press. Nevertheless, the popular concept of the Moonies is, according to George Robertson, their press officer, that they are a malign group of crazed, brainwashing lunatics, who capture young minds and turn them into vegetables. He adds: 'The reality is that we are a normal group of people on a spiritual path, looking to improve the world.' Although Barker concedes that misinformation, and manipulation may occur to new converts of new religious movements, she raises questions about the efficacy of this manipulation, pointing out that the vast majority leave them in a matter of years.

The crux of the debate between academics and cultwatch groups centres on the concept of 'brainwashing' or 'mind control'. Families, exit counsellors and journalists working in the area will tell stories of countless instances of mind control. They will produce examples of individuals who have left cults and re-entered normal life, and who appear to have rediscovered their personalities again. In short, the converts who caused such disquiet among family and friends, after conversion have reverted to type, but also to behaviours which seem more natural, relaxed and genuine. They claim to have been manipulated into losing their way to the extent that they have let go of the responsibility for making their own decisions, and have become automatons for the cult.

Academics generally will have none of it. In *New Religious Movements: a practical introduction* Eileen Barker says: 'One of the most popular explanations that is given for people joining a NRM is that they have been brainwashed or have undergone some kind of "mind control" There are various reasons for the popularity of such an explanation, not the least of which is that it tends to absolve everyone (apart from the NRM in question) from any kind of responsibility.' She rejects the idea that people can have their minds controlled, suggesting that people give up responsibility for their own decisions voluntarily, and that this is a decision in itself. Whilst accepting that new religious movements may manipulate potential converts by 'love bombing', use of guilt and deceptive information, she points out that if the techniques are genuinely meant to control minds, they fail miserably. Concerning Michael Howard's 'sinister' Moonies, Barker's research shows that only 0.1 % of people who had visited Unification Centres were members a year after their visit. She also points to studies of voluntary defectors from new religious movements who, she say, 'are extremely unlikely to believe that they were ever a victim of mind control.'

So how did NOS manage to attract and control hundreds of intelligent people for so long? Paul Heelas, Reader in Religion and Modernity at Lancaster University, points out that 'mind control' is a misnomer, but believes that it is possible for charismatic religious leaders to exert considerable influence on their followers. Although there is no simple formula for conversion to a new religious movement or cult, Heelas stresses it is as important to consider the agenda of the converts as well as the 'intensive socialisation' (which some would call manipulation and deception) and psychological techniques used by the leader.

One factor is the attractiveness of the group's cultural plausibility (this could be NOS's street cum club culture or the popularity of its professed social action and save-the-planet agenda). NOS was made up of liberal minded and radical people seeking an 'alternative' within the Christian tradition. Another factor that Heelas highlights is an awareness on the part of members that 'life isn't working as well as it should' and, for the disillusioned refugees from the evangelical, charismatic church this is surely true in relation to their faith. Participants having 'intense out-of-the-ordinary experiences' is another possible determinant and surely most NOS services offered participants just this. Heelas stresses that there are likely to be other 'social psychological processes' that are operative. For NOS members, the affirming inclusiveness of the grassroots community will have been significant. Paradoxically, so too will the NOS hierarchy's power structures, and the culture of secrecy, fear and alienation.

It also has to be pointed out that NOS members weren't a representative cross section of society. More significant than the fact that many members were middle class educated, young professionals is the fact that the majority were disillusioned evangelicals and charismatics. They had therefore already had a conversion experience which they considered deeply meaningful but which they felt hadn't been matched by their experience of the Church. Charismatics, with their emphasis on the supernatural and miraculous, are notoriously open to alleged touches of the supernatural in their lives. But disillusioned charismatics, holding to a precious and deeply felt experience, are more likely to be eager to embrace uncritically a meaningful reinterpretation of their experience which breathes new life into it. Brain had a captive audience, in many ways, desperate for what he had to offer. The mixture of his intense, single-minded and charismatic personality and his radical, idealistic reinterpretation of evangelical, charismatic Christianity was irresistible. The vision covered a multitude of sins and claimed people's loyalty long after they started asking questions about abusive behaviours. After all where is there to go for *disillusioned*, disillusioned charismatics?

The NOS vision should not be denigrated simply because of its association with abusive practices. It is possible to detach the vision from its founder's failings and the experiences associated with it, even if many of the experiences directly contradict the vision. A church standing against sexism, poverty, greed, abuse of power and environmental catastrophe is surely no bad thing. A church seeking to engage with art and culture, seeking to communicate in a challenging and creative way to postmodern society probably has much to offer. Many outsiders and members on the periphery found it the most meaningful, vibrant and relevant form of Christianity they had ever come across. The vision, in isolation, was 'positive' and as such had integrity as a factor which persuaded members to stick with it. It is partly a testimony to the depth of their commitment that they stayed with it for so long. Ultimately the pain and the contradictions within the service became too much and members had to ask themselves uncomfortable questions and actively take back their autonomy and expose the reality of the abuse.

To say that many NOS members were experiencing a lot of pain is understatement. Indeed, the situations in which they found themselves, mirrored the descriptions of potentially dangerous and abusive cults provided by both academics and cult watchers. Eileen Barker's list of 'potentially dangerous situations' in which members of new religious movements may find themselves, warns people of the following:

1) A movement cutting itself off (either geographically or socially) from the rest of society.

2) A convert becoming increasingly dependent on the movement for definition and testing of 'reality'.

3) A movement drawing sharp, unnegotiable boundaries between 'them' and 'us', 'godly' and 'satanic', 'good' and 'bad'— and so on.

4) Important decisions about converts' lives being made for them by others.

5) Leaders claiming divine authority for their actions and their demands.

6) Leaders or movements pursuing a single goal in a single-minded manner.' (Ref. 1)

Another check-list also sheds light on the situation in NOS. This list is from a less impartial source but, like Barker's list, it is based on the experiences of members of abusive religious organisations. Published by the Christian based Spiritual Counterfeits Project in Berkeley, California, it is aimed at Christians who may be in 'cult-like' churches and is written from a Christian standpoint. Once again, in many ways it is a description of members' experiences at

NOS. Under the title *Twelve Characteristics of a Counterfeit Church/Cult*, the list points to the following factors:

1) Authoritarian, oppressive leadership; no room for other ideas and independent action.

2) Lack of accountability at the top; leaders don't need or want to answer for their actions.

3) Pyramid of power; the further from the top, the less power and influence members have.

4) Belief that members and their families are inferior to the leader and his circle.

5) Belief that the leader is closer to God and can hear Him better than the lay people.

6) Strong pressure to conform to the manner, dress, speech, et cetera of those in power.

7) Financial needs of the group (or its leaders) placed above those of members' families.

8) Pressure to give undue amounts of time to the group, to neglect other responsibilities.

9) An 'us-versus-them' mentality; distrust of all other churches/groups/persuasions.

10) Narrow doctrines and teachings so unique that only this group has the 'right path'.

11) Discouragement of frank and open discussion about the group, its doctrine, or its leaders.

12) Ostracism of former members; prejudice against those no longer 'choosing to belong'. (ref. 2)

Not all NOS members would call it a cult, but they would generally say that it was cult-like. Proximity to Brain was a major factor which would make people see it as a cult. Those holding responsibilities, involved in Homebase or giving much of their time to NOS would almost invariably refer to NOS as a cult. Some of the older members were treated with more respect and they would say that it was cult-like. Conversely there are new members (and people on the periphery) who hadn't had sufficient time to see the abuses and manipulations, who are still bemused about why it collapsed amid such angst. The membership selection process filtered out the less committed, and this meant that members tended to give their whole lives to it. This accounts for the number who call it a cult with such certainty.

But exactly when a church becomes a cult is a question which needs addressing. It is ironic that an organisation that was displaying some of the most abusive characteristics of 'cults' was in fact a fully fledged, if experimental, part of the Church of England. But surely it is also true that conventional churches often display some cult-like characteristics too. Many churches, for instance, have authoritarian leadership, a strong pressure to conform to group norms and to spend large amounts of time in church activities, and discourage frank and open discussion. The change from church to cult is probably a continuum, a question of degree. It may well be easier for church groups to become 'cults' because some of the characteristics are already in place. It could also be argued that because NOS was purportedly challenging traditional authority structures, people felt insecure and hence, paradoxically, depended on leaders to a much greater extent than is normal.

Sociologists normally distinguish quite clearly between churches and cults (often described as sects). Writing in the 1930s, Ernst Troeltsch was one of the first sociologists to distinguish different types of religious organisations. He used the term 'church' to describe large religious organisations which are closely related to the state and in which members do not have to demonstrate their faith, they are often born into it. Members are free to play a full part in social life and because churches accept and affirm life in this world, there is no pressure to withdraw from society. Churches are ideologically conservative and usually support the status quo. Churches differ from 'denominations' in that denominations don't have nearly such broad appeal in wider society and don't accept any alignment with the state; they may well have minor differences with wider society on issues such as gambling or alcohol but they generally accept the norms and values of society. Troeltsch's understanding of sects is that they are diametrically opposed to churches.

A sect is on a much smaller scale than a church and its members' lives are much more closely integrated. Sects will tend to be opposed to the values of wider society and may withdraw from society and/or lobby for change. Members of sects choose to join voluntarily and must demonstrate a strong commitment to the sect's values, lifestyle and beliefs. They must be willing to forego some of the pleasures offered by wider society. With the explosion of sects in recent years, however, more detailed analyses of sects or new religious movements have been carried out.

The late Roy Wallis, Professor of Sociology at Queen's University, Belfast, described three main types whilst acknowledging that there are some groups which don't fit neatly into his categories. His categories are: 'World-rejecting sects' (such as the Moonies, ISKCON or Hare Krishna or David Koresh's Branch Davidians); 'world accommodating sects' (the neo-pentecostal groups such as the house churches); and 'world affirming' sects (such as Transcendental Meditation and self improvement 'therapy cults' like Est or Scientology). In essence, world accommodating sects tend to focus purely on the spiritual and see the world as neutral or irrelevant, world affirming sects tend to use the spiritual as a means of succeeding in the world, whereas world rejecting sects are a fusion between a pronounced spirituality and a radical, idealistic and sometimes iconoclastic approach to the world.

Within ten years, NOS moved from being a part of the conservative, if liberal minded Church of England, (a symbol of everything safe, homely and traditional) to what appears to be a world rejecting religious sect. Andrew Walker, Lecturer in Theology and Education at King's College, London, believes that this cultic 'implant' was possible because of the woolly-minded liberalism of the Church of England. He says: 'If you have a broad based liberal religious organisation which isn't very good at monitoring its activities, it is an ideal structure within which more extreme, exclusive and idealistic groups can flourish.' That the laissez faire ethos of the Anglican establishment allowed NOS to happen is borne out by Brain, who said when I interviewed him five years ago: 'It is the wishy washiness of the Anglican Church which has given us the freedom for these new things to come about. This liberal approach could be the jewel in the Church's crown, rather than something to worry about.'

However, according to Walker there is no inevitability that abuse takes place in groups with a strong spiritual ethic and values that run counter to outside culture. Pointing to the Quakers and black Christian anti-apartheid activists in South Africa as examples of healthy yet alternative spirituality, Walker believes that there are two key factors which may affect the counter cultural religious groups for the worse. The use and abuse of power is, in his view, the key determinant. Leaders who are continually seeking to shed their power and to implement democratic structures are highly unlikely to create abusive systems. Another related but less obvious factor is the extent to which such groups dialogue openly with the world whose values they are questioning. A group which arrogantly or defensively (or both) rejects the world can only become increasingly insular and more entrenched and narrow in its attitudes. An openness to dialogue and relationship naturally makes it far less likely that members are going to create a dangerously isolated parallel universe.

Sheffield's archdeacon, Stephen Lowe, also believes that 'alternative worship' was not responsible for the NOS debacle. In the diocese's report on NOS to the Archbishop, they suggest changes of church practice which could help avoid such events in the future. They argue for some form of personality profiling of the type used in industry before people are accepted for ordination, to be followed up by professional supervision of their relationships with individuals, drawing on the expertise of psychotherapists and social workers. They also say that no church should exist without a democratically elected church council. Finally they believe that bishops and archdeacons need greater accountability from priests; they need to have the right in church law to challenge them to account for their conduct as ministers. These recommendations apart, Lowe shares the Archbishop of Canterbury's well-known enthusiasm for alternative worship groups.

The 'Late Service' is a Glasgow based alternative worship group of about 70 members which has been running for several years. Originating from a group of artists who felt ill at ease with their evangelical and charismatic heritage, they decided to experiment with worship and community. Andy Thornton, one of the founder members, explains that they wanted to create worship which reflected their culture: 'We were looking for an authentic worship with which we could seek to relate to God. Our 'vision' is that simple: to live with integrity and to love God.' They use dance music and multi-media film techniques because that is an expression of the culture in which they live.

Thornton stresses that the quality of relationships is the key: 'For us the Way is more important than the Vision. We want to celebrate diversity rather than impose a way of operating which others will fit into.' They have democratic structures which involve shared responsibility and a steering group that is based on a rota. 'When new people join', Thornton says, 'we want our worship and our practices to adapt to accommodate them, we want to learn from them; there is not one correct method that will work for all, and we want a repertoire of spiritual exercises and worship practices which work for the whole community.'

To some extent Late Service values are counter culture. Thornton says: 'We certainly want to stand against sexism and the callous treatment of the poor and marginalised in our society but we're mindful of what we can do as a congregation; we'd rather work with other agencies than go it alone.' The radical nature of their ideas is also fuelled by their faith but as active members of the local ecumenical Council of Churches they want to learn from others within and outside the Church. 'There will never be a day that we feel that we have got the answers; we are trying to find solutions by living creatively and reflecting a creative God, but central to this is an openness to others and a willingness to learn', Thornton says.

 'Holy Joes' is another radical church group that meets each week in a pub in Clapham. The leader, Dave Tomlinson, has a heritage which has made him particularly suspicious of power and of grand claims about the supernatural. Fifteen years ago he resigned from the leadership of a network of charismatic house churches because of what he saw as abuses of power and control within the movement. 'I felt deeply unhappy with the obedience that pastors demanded of their membership and felt that it was a long way from the heart of Christianity; it was offering members little choice in terms of theology, ideology and lifestyle and young people had to conform to a very conventional outlook which many of them felt ill at ease with', Tomlinson now says. He adds: 'Being in leadership I could only question the much vaunted miracles that we were claiming and promising; they simply never happened.'

Because of this Holy Joes was set up with a loose leadership in which Tomlinson functioned as facilitator of a group of disillusioned Christians, often chairing anarchic discussions about Christianity in relation to contemporary issues in society. About 30 people came and pastoral and personal issues were dealt with informally through friendship groups.' The central aim of Holy Joes was to do with making sense of our faith in the modern world. For many it acted as a sanctuary from what they experienced as an abusive church', Tomlinson says. Holy Joes is definitely critical of the Church and much in society but maintained strong links with similar groups and was deliberately inclusive in its outlook. 'We are there to take on anyone's agenda and to try and further our understanding and experience of faith', Tomlinson explains.

Tomlinson believes that because society has undergone a major cultural shift (which might be termed postmodernism in that people no longer believe in over-arching explanations of the human condition, whether religious, scientific or psychological), the attempt of the religious communities simply to reassert the old 'certainties' will fail. He sees the relative success of the evangelical/charismatic church as largely a defensive reaction to uncertainty whilst believing that it is possible to have a real faith in God. He suggests that a new approach is needed because both the liberal theological approach and the charismatic one are based in modernism — liberalism is an accommodation of modernism and evangelical charismaticism is a reaction to it. 'A middle way which includes rational questioning as well as a belief in mystery is surely the way forward and this is at the heart of the alternative worship groups', he says.

Tomlinson believes that the experiences at NOS will not prove wholly negative, since their agenda was highly pertinent for the rest of the Church. 'Their theological and pastoral problems had nothing to do with their aims; it was the fundamentalist, dogmatic approach to their aims as implemented by Chris Brain that seemed to create the problems', he says. 'There are things to learn not just from what went wrong at NOS but more positively from the issues that they were addressing', he says, adding: 'If these issues are approached with humility, openness and love, then the whole Church could benefit.'

Notes

Ref. 1 - Barker, E., 1989, *New Religious Movements*, HMSO.
Ref. 2 - Mr Charles Leeser SCP Newsletter,16:2 1992, *Is Your Church Cult-like?*

DATE DUE

'2 2 NOV 2004			

Demco, Inc. 38-293